Great Minds Don't Think Alike!

Success for Students through the Application

of Psychological Type in Schools

DIANE PAYNE AND SONDRA VANSANT

C A P T

Center for Applications of Psychological Type, Inc. · 2815 NW 13th St., Suite 401 · Gainesville, FL 32609 · 1.800.777.2278 · www.capt.org

Published by
Center for Applications of Psychological Type
2815 NW 13th St., Suite 401
Gainesville, FL 32609
www.capt.org

Library of Congress Cataloging-in-Publication Data

Payne, Diane, 1942-
    Great minds don't think alike! : success for students through the application of psychological type in schools / Diane Payne and Sondra VanSant.
        p. cm.
    Includes bibliographical references and index.
    ISBN 978-0-935652-88-8 (pbk. : alk. paper)
1. Learning, Psychology of. 2. Typology (Psychology) 3. Cognitive styles. I. VanSant, Sondra. II. Title.
    LB1060.P396 2009
    370.15'23--dc22

2009030753

Printed in the United States of America.

DEDICATIONS

to Mike, my rock – dp

to Jerry for love, patience, and joy – sv

Table of Contents

Acknowledgments ix

Preface xi

Introduction xv

Chapter 1

PERSONALITY TYPE: THE BASICS 1

C.G. Jung's Types as Adapted by Isabel Myers 2
The Preferences Explained 3
From Preferences to Personality Types 12
To Wrap it Up 15
In a Nutshell 15
Check Your Understanding 15

Chapter 2

PERSONALIZING INSTRUCTION 19

Personalize Words of Instruction 20
Personalize Learning Activities 22
Direct Instruction and Type 30
Time Management and Work Habits 35
Should Students and Teachers Be Matched by Type? 41
To Wrap it Up 41
In a Nutshell 41
Check Your Understanding 42
Getting Started 43

Chapter 3

PERSONALIZING THE LEARNING ENVIRONMENT 45

Optimal Learning Environment 45
Use of Physical Space 47
Negotiating "Learning Community" Space 49
Managing Student Behavior 49
Preventing Discipline Problems 51
To Wrap it Up 58
In a Nutshell 58
Check Your Understanding 59
Getting Started 60

Chapter 4

PERSONALIZING ASSESSMENT 61

Developing Criteria for Evaluation 61

Accommodating Type Differences in Assessment 63

Student Centered Self-Assessment 63

Portfolio Assessment 67

Teacher-Designed Tests 70

Standardized Testing 76

Type and GPA 83

To Wrap it Up 84

In a Nutshell 84

Check Your Understanding 85

Getting Started 86

Chapter 5

PERSONALIZING PATHWAYS TO ACHIEVEMENT 87

Early Development of Type 87

Later Development of Type 91

School Is Important for Type Development 92

Helping Underachieving Students Develop Strengths 92

Type and Intelligence 94

Teachers Can Begin with Personalized Instruction 95

General Guidelines to Promote Type Development in the Classroom 95

To Wrap it Up 104

In a Nutshell 104

Check Your Understanding 104

Getting Started 106

Chapter 6

COLLABORATION IN TEAMS 107

Bringing Psychological Type to the Table 108

Determining Team Strengths and Potential Difficulties 109

Case Studies for Team Work 110

To Wrap it Up 118

In a Nutshell 118

Check Your Understanding 119

Getting Started 120

Chapter 7

COLLABORATION IN DECISION MAKING AND PROBLEM SOLVING 121

Strategies Used for Decision Making by Type Preferences 123

Strategies Used for Problem Solving by Type Preferences 124

Problem-Solving Strategies of School Principals 126

Application of Problem-Solving Strategies 127

To Wrap it Up 130

In a Nutshell 130

Check Your Understanding 131

Getting Started 131

Chapter 8

COLLABORATION IN CONFLICT MANAGEMENT 133

Conflict Resolution Styles 133

How the Types Respond to Conflict 138

Using Type to Understand and Resolve Conflict 138

Type Differences in Conflict 140

To Wrap it Up 148

In a Nutshell 148

Check Your Understanding 149

Getting Started 151

Chapter 9

COLLABORATION IN SCHOOL OPERATIONS 153

Recognizing Achievements and Accomplishments 154

Giving Support and Encouragement 157

Determining Responsibility for Tasks 159

Handling Disagreements and Difficulties 163

Improving Meetings 167

Improving the Work Environment 169

To Wrap it Up 170

In a Nutshell 170

Check Your Understanding 171

Getting Started 172

Chapter 10

INTRODUCING TYPE IN SCHOOLS 174

Professional Development 174

Advice for the Qualified Trainer 174

Administration of the MBTI® Instrument 175

Type Workshop Agenda 176

Follow-up 177

Role of the Principal 177

Teacher Colleagues as Consultants 178

Communicating Preferences 179

First Things First: Value Your Own Type! 179

To Wrap it Up 180

In a Nutshell 180

Check Your Understanding 181

Getting Started 181

Appendix

Type Table: Teachers, Elementary School 182

Type Table: Teachers, Middle School 183

Type Table: Teachers, Secondary School 183

National Distribution of Types 185

Endnotes 186

Bibliography 186

List of Resources

Introduction to Resources 193

Acknowledgments

It takes a team, or a book doesn't get written. To our surprise, producing a second edition was in some ways more involved than writing the first, and we are doubly grateful to our team of generous colleagues, friends, and family for their significant contributions of expertise, editing, and inspiration. We have learned from each of them.

There have been additional students, teachers, and education leaders in the intervening years since the last edition whose knowledge and insights have confirmed and expanded our understanding of how to use psychological type for more effective learning in schools. The excellent teachers who originally contributed, and in some cases for this edition revisited the curriculum samples, include Jimmy Baker, Margaret Brown, Nancy Cheek, Nancy Clark, Elizabeth Clarkson, Beth Lineberger, Lynne Misenheimer, Ann Overton, Vicki Overton, Helen Roberts, Bill Rucker, and Benton Satterfield. Lynn Lee joined this group with advice on math questions. Barry and Denise O'Sullivan gave us invaluable feedback from their experience with use of the first edition in classrooms and education research in Australia. Barry's comments were our inspiration for the "Getting Started" sections of each chapter. Denise's research influenced our decision to put additional focus on the impact of Sensing and Intuition in the learning process.

Louis Fabrizio, director of the Division of Accountability Services for the North Carolina Department of Public Instruction, again gave us permission to include released, sample test-items from state End of Grade and End of Course tests for the section on type and assessment.

Of course, the team of diverse minds at the Center for Applications of Psychological Type made it all possible. Essential has been the encouragement of Betsy Styron, CEO, who recommended this second edition as an accompaniment to the fine work of Elizabeth Murphy and Charles Meisgeier on the Murphy-Meisgeier Type Indicator for Children® (MMTIC®) assessment. With CAPT's publication of the new MMTIC assessment, there is now an instrument to help students from elementary through high school identify their type. Eleanor K. Sommer's wise counsel and high standards as our editor required us to raise our own standards for clarity and practical application. We can only imagine the tedium as she plowed through the first drafts. Naima Cortes as project director navigated us through the system already filled with works waiting to be published. Jamie Johnson, who continues to be a storehouse of knowledge about where just about anything important is and how to find it, once again directed us correctly to publishing and research information we needed. John Amerson and Gina Smith of the production department infused energy and interest into the cover and each page of words with their graphics and suggestion of pictures and quotes from well-known "great minds."

Last but by no means least we recognize those wise and great minds of C. G. Jung and Isabel Myers whose understanding of how the human mind informs itself and makes decisions remains a solid foundation even as technology they never knew makes possible the explosion of new discoveries by current great minds in the neurosciences. Sitting in thousands of classrooms around the globe are young minds eagerly preparing to join them.

Diane Payne and Sondra VanSant

Preface to the Second Edition

Leadership and learning are indispensable to each other.

JOHN F. KENNEDY

I never let my schooling get in the way of my education," Mark Twain proudly proclaimed as he sent his free-spirited Huckleberry Finn and other characters on a raft down the Mississippi River. Of course, Twain wasn't the only well-known achiever to either detest or fail at formal schooling. For every Samuel Clemmons, Albert Einstein, and Thomas Edison, there are thousands of young people dropping out of school each year who do *not* succeed in achieving their potential in life. It is for these dropouts, as well as for those who hang in there but feel out of place in the school setting, that numerous school reforms have been proposed for all levels of the educational system. National and state leaders, government officials, educational leaders, parents, and others are searching for ways to raise achievement for all students.

A little over a decade ago when we wrote *Psychological Type in Schools: Applications for Educators,* we set out to answer two questions: "How can knowledge of personality type make a difference in schools?" and "What do educators need that is not already available to help them apply type to their work in schools?" To answer the first question, we used data we had collected from the types on how they best learn, demonstrate their knowledge, and stay focused in the classroom. We answered the second question by including "how-to" material that we discovered was absent from most of the literature at the time. Now more than ten years later after numerous conversations with teachers, administrators, and students, we find the same two questions still compelling. Thus we have written this update to address the continuing need for a "how-to" book on type and learning.

Changes in Education

Dramatic changes have occurred in education in the last decade. Charter schools have emerged as an alternative to traditional public schools; the number of families who home school their children has exploded; and stakes have been raised with the use of standardized test results for student promotion, graduation, and school-funding decisions. Learning activities in the classroom are more varied with greater emphasis on individualized and experiential learning. Many high schools now operate with block scheduling and require students to complete senior projects or to be involved in community service as requirements for graduation.

Classroom demographics have shifted and schools now have many more students for whom English is a second language. Computer technology, which had limited availability a decade ago, is now regarded as an essential component of learning in most schools. The Internet has opened the world as a classroom. Today, happily, we observe that experiential learning is much more customary in schools and the classroom is much larger than the space defined by four walls. The federal government has assumed a more active role in determining what happens in schools, and state governments are major players.

Changes in Book Content

After the request to write a second edition, we asked colleagues in education, other authors, and former workshop participants for recommendations about the contents of a new edition. Teachers and trainers told us how they adapted instructions and lessons to engage the diversity of minds present in their classrooms. Principals told us they use type to strengthen staff relations and to coach teachers on how to increase student engagement. Parents shared successful experiences about how they use the handbook to understand their children better and to talk with their children's teachers about how their children learn. As parents ourselves we are aware of the deep frustration that occurs when a child and a teacher do not connect. We have also experienced the joy that comes when type helps make that connection.

We have made additions and changes in this new version as a result of the recommendations and suggestions we received. We have included information on basic type concepts rather than assume all our readers are already familiar with Carl Jung's and Isabel Myers' work. We have added a summary for each chapter along with suggestions for getting started with that chapter's content. We even added a brief quiz for readers to check their understanding of the content of each chapter (with the answers to the questions, of course!). We have also expanded the section on introducing type in schools. Readers of this volume who are familiar with the first edition will find major revisions to every chapter—some content incorporates richer knowledge of type and learning and some reflects changes in schools today.

Intended Audience

This book is for educators in all settings. To us that includes teachers in public and private school classrooms from kindergarten to twelfth grade, parents who work collaboratively with teachers for their children to be successfully engaged in learning, parents who home school their children, principals and other school administrators who provide leadership and organization appropriate for the educational enterprise, and those educators and trainers who teach those who teach the students and lead the schools. Trainers of adults in a variety of settings, as well as those involved in instructional design will find materials useful for their work.

As educators deal with the many challenges they face today, we believe the incorporation of personality type as a tool for personalization and collaboration leads to success for students. Schools become true professional learning communities when collaboration is embedded in the culture of the school and routinely becomes "the way we do things around here." When everyone in the school community works collaboratively students are engaged and good things happen. Engaged students will not even entertain the idea of dropping out of school!

Diane Payne and Sondra VanSant

Introduction: Focus and Organization of Contents

Contents focus on personalized learning and collaborative leadership and can be summarized as follows:

Chapter 1 explains personality type.

Chapters 2–5 apply personality type to personalized learning.

Chapters 6–9 apply personality type to collaborative leadership.

Chapter 10 describes how to introduce personality type in schools.

A Brief Description of Each Chapter

Chapter 1, "Personality Type: The Basics," gives an overview with school-based examples of Carl Jung's cognitive functions and attitudes that are the basis for type, including Isabel Myers' adaptation that produces sixteen types.

Chapter 2, "Personalizing Instruction," focuses on engaging and motivating students from the introduction of a new learning objective through the teacher's choice of words for instruction and learning activities, as well as differences in time management. The chapter includes specific examples gathered from the types and a step-by-step illustration of a lesson designed to engage different types.

Chapter 3, "Personalizing the Learning Environment," covers the physical and learning climate in which the types learn best and has recommendations for use of classroom space and managing student behavior.

Chapter 4, "Personalizing Assessment," makes the case and provides tools for ongoing student assessment that reflects "real world" skills as well as application of type differences to student-centered self-assessment, portfolio assessment, teacher-designed tests, and standardized testing.

Chapter 5, "Personalizing Pathways to Achievement," explains how achievement can be increased when students are encouraged to engage their naturally dominant preferences first and then over time support these preferences with the remaining mental functions and attitudes. Tools and strategies are provided for helping students find their pathways to achievement.

Chapter 6, "Collaboration in Teams," includes discussion of the benefits for groups and teams of using type, tools for team diagnosis and analysis, and case studies illustrating ways to increase collaborative team effectiveness.

Chapter 7, "Collaboration in Decision Making and Problem Solving," gives examples of strategies for decision making and problem solving by type preferences and illustrates how type differences affect the way people view situations and approach problem solving. Type-specific tips for problem solving are also provided.

Chapter 8, "Collaboration in Conflict Management," presents the central idea that people's approach to understanding and dealing with conflict is in some measure related to their personality types. The chapter includes a description of five conflict resolution styles along with examples and ways to use type to understand and resolve conflicts.

Chapter 9, "Collaboration in School Operations," provides information and examples to illustrate effective ways of working with people in the daily operation of schools. In addition to providing specific ways type can be helpful in areas such as staff recognition, providing support and encouragement, and the assignment of tasks and responsibilities, the chapter includes suggestions for conducting effective meetings and handling disagreements.

Chapter 10, "Introducing Type in Schools," provides specific suggestions for finding formal and informal opportunities to introduce type into schools as well as suggestions and an agenda for a professional development workshop.

Following these chapters, to support your use of personality type in schools, you will find reproducible resources as well as an appendix of charts indicating type distributions in school populations. The resources section is generous and includes lesson plans with details for using type with various subjects including math, science, social studies, and English.

Personality Type: The Basics

"To each his own" is the old saying now modernized as "different strokes for different folks." To achieve the intent of these sayings will take a lot of work in coming to see our differences as something other than flaws.

DAVID KIERSEY, *Please Understand Me*

Teacher Sara Jones has every intention of connecting with the minds of José, Susan, Bob, Shawndra, and her other twenty-two students as she begins a language arts lesson. The objective for the lesson she is teaching states that students will be able to express their individuals points of view in writing. Sara has prepared an assignment she believes each student can relate to and accomplish and one that will provide material for students to self-critique for reader interest, use of language, and grammatical construction.

Sara introduces her assignment by saying: "I would like for you to imagine yourself as an adult who is working in a job you love. Then write an essay of no more than 500 words on what your typical day is like and why it is so satisfying."

Instantly, her students' minds react. If only Sara could read their minds, she might hear internal commentary such as the following:

José: Cool! I like doing this.

Susan: Not again! What does this have to do with anything real?

Bob: Another no-brainer. What a waste of time!

Shawndra: Uh! Oh! Susan and Bob look like they're going to give

Mrs. Jones a hard time again.

Sara, with all good intention, has connected in the way she planned—but with only one of these four students.

As an educator, you know it is something of a miracle for a teacher to connect with *all* her students, especially in today's world where so many competing priorities and issues confront students. You are very aware, we're sure, how staggering the array of these issues can be, as each child represents an entirely different amalgam of biological systems, inherited traits, personality factors, family heritage, cultural norms, and faith experiences—none of which a teacher can control. Yet despite being faced with these issues, a teacher's task is to engage *each* child in the learning process. We believe it is in the area of connecting and engaging students personally that the teacher *can* have some control, *can* catch the attention of each student and engage that mind in such a way that motivation kicks in and the student takes charge of his or her own learning.

So how could Sara better understand how her words of instruction engaged or disengaged her students? How could she determine that José's mind immediately connected positively with "imagine yourself," while these same words were immediate turn-offs for the other three—possibly too irrelevant to Susan, too personal to Bob, too unimaginable for Shawndra, who focused instead on something with which she had first-hand experience (in this case, watching the frequent troublemaking of Susan and Bob)? Knowing the answer would have given Sara a great deal of control over her ability to connect with these students' minds.

C. G. Jung's Types as Adapted by Isabel Briggs Myers

One model that provides some answers and has stood the test of time and research in explaining how people learn and perform at their highest level is the "personality type" theory of Swiss psychiatrist Carl G. Jung. Katharine Briggs and Isabel Briggs Myers adapted and extended Jung's work and developed the Myers-Briggs Type Indicator® (MBTI®) instrument to make Jung's model more accessible to individuals in their everyday lives. For more than fifty years, many organizations, including schools, have incorporated Jung's and Myers' ideas about type into their daily functioning, demonstrably contributing to higher levels of performance. (Throughout this book, we will use the word "type" to refer to the set of ideas contained in Jung's and Myers' work with typology.)

The type model explains how people use their minds in equally good but very different ways to take in information and make decisions. According to this model, our minds incorporate four innate dichotomies when seeking understanding and making decisions. One pole of each dichotomy, also known as a "preference," is more natural for each of us and use of its opposite requires more concentrated effort.

Figure 1.1 *Chart of Basic Preferences*

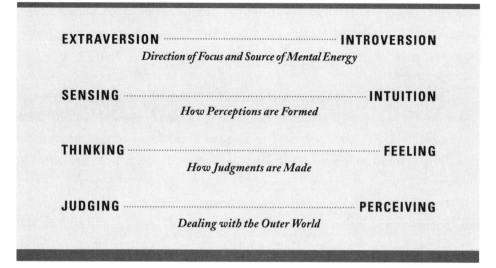

EXTRAVERSION ························· INTROVERSION
Direction of Focus and Source of Mental Energy

SENSING ························· INTUITION
How Perceptions are Formed

THINKING ························· FEELING
How Judgments are Made

JUDGING ························· PERCEIVING
Dealing with the Outer World

The preferences are access points for the mind and provide the "trigger" to engage the mind. The key to engaging students, therefore, is to understand these equally good but opposite preferences and offer the kinds of learning opportunities that give all students a chance to work with their *natural* preferences.

And the question, of course, is "How does a teacher do this?" Chapter 2 will answer this question directly, but first, let's talk more about what these opposite preferences actually mean.

The Preferences Explained

Just as most people are born with a predisposition to more naturally prefer using one hand over the other, people are also hardwired with a natural tendency to prefer one of the two opposite poles on each of the four dichotomies, according to Jung. Natural preferences are developed over time from the interaction of innate hardwiring and environmental reinforcement, while the opposite preferences assume valuable supportive roles. (Please note that Jung did not capitalize any of the preferences, but when they are used in relationship to the MBTI instrument developed by Isabel Myers, the eight preferences are proper nouns.)

Extraversion and Introversion: Direction of Focus and Source of Mental Energy

Jung uses the words Extraversion and Introversion to indicate a *direction and source of mental energy*. People's energy can be focused away from themselves to the outer environment—a direction Jung called *extraversion*, or toward an inner environment within themselves—a direction he called *introversion*. (Yes, Jung did invent those words, which is why we use the "a," as he did, to spell *extraversion*.) These directions of energy are critical factors for student learning in the classroom because they explain where an individual's mental energy is activated and replenished.

Everyone's attention is drawn at various times to both the outer (extraverted) and inner (introverted) environments. However, connecting with one of these environments is mentally energizing to some of us while for others, after briefly providing some refreshing balance, this same direction of energy becomes mentally draining.

People for whom the external environment is more often energizing direct their energy frequently outward to the world of people, objects, and actions, the direction called *extraversion*. Others more naturally draw their mental energy from their inner world of ideas and reflections, the direction called *introversion*.

Extraversion and Introversion in the Classroom

In the classroom, students with a preference for Extraversion are usually sociable and like to learn through action or interaction; they typically want limited instructions so they can get on with their learning by *doing* something as quickly as possible. Their sequence of learning often involves trying something out, reflecting on their experience, and then trying it out again.

Students with a preference for Introversion usually like to reflect first to make sure they have a thorough understanding of the instructions and task. Their sequence of learning is to reflect, and then try something out, followed by further reflection.

This suggests the need for choices as to which environment is the most effective for a student to begin a learning activity. In our earlier example, Sara could have suggested or provided choices for her writing assignment to include both Extraversion and Introversion and therefore have engaged both kinds of minds. Assigning students to hold conversations with adults or using online sites and other resources and working with a classmate would have tapped into Extraversion. Assigning students to read books, magazines, or online sites individually would tap into Introversion.

Sensing and Intuition: How Perceptions Are Formed

Perception, as defined by Jung, deals with what information most attracts the mind and then, once engaged, how the mind utilizes this information to form a perception. These opposite ways of perceiving are known as Sensing (or sensation as Jung called the term) and Intuition. While everyone uses both Sensing and Intuition, one of them is a person's *natural* preference and thus the way a person's mind is most easily engaged.

Sensing attends to specific, concrete information that can be verified with an experience of the moment or from an experience in the past. Think of using the five senses—something is real because you can taste it, touch it, hear it, see it, or smell it. Sensing gives form to discrete pieces of information gathered from experience by putting them together in a structured way, ideally for a practical application. Sensing provides an understanding of "what is."

For example, if a person hangs a new picture on the wall, a mind with Sensing engaged will notice the specifics of the picture—the texture, color, individual people or pieces that make up the whole, the number and size of objects, whether the picture is framed, and if it is hanging straight or not.

People with a preference for Sensing, therefore, are engaged more easily by reality, not imagination or abstraction; by solid fact, not theory; by the *pieces* of information, not a global concept. With a grasp of the concrete specifics first in any given situation ("what is"), these minds then can be stimulated to see new possibilities in the future ("what could be"). This shift in focus leads to the opposite perception preference, which is Intuition.

Intuition does not attend to the specifics but to the *meaning* of the specifics —to that "sixth sense"—those hunches, inspirations, understandings that come to a person in the moment. Intuition's focus is on the big picture, on patterns, themes, and relationships. A mind engaged with Intuition is interested in possibilities of the moment or the future and would rather deal with "what could be" than "what is."

So in our example of that picture on the wall, a person whose mind is engaged with Intuition is likely to form a general impression of the picture. This person may look for a theme or associate it with similar pictures but not notice the specifics of the picture, let alone notice if it is hanging straight or not!

People whose preference is Intuition are drawn to imagination and new possibilities in the moment or in the future, not to factual information; they are also drawn to symbols and metaphors, to patterns and associations, but not to discrete pieces of data. Their minds make tangential associations that to them are related to the matter at hand, though others may not see the relationship. They are most easily engaged first with the big picture so that they have a context for then grasping the specific pieces needed to make the possibility work. They are quickly bored with anything that seems obvious.

Sensing and Intuition in the Classroom

Now consider the instructions Sara gave her class. "I would like for you to *imagine . . . .*"Those of her students who have a natural preference for Sensing are not likely to be engaged easily by the word *imagine*, as it does not relate to something real as defined by concrete, known information about the present or past. Sara's Sensing students are likely to appreciate the specific parameter she gave of a 500-word maximum, but this parameter will be of little value to them if the words of introduction to the assignment have not motivated them to undertake the task. For students with a preference for Sensing, Sara might have said something like this: "I would like for you to gather information on at least three jobs people do and choose one that interests you the most. Then describe in writing, using no more than 500 words, what a typical working day is like for people in that field. Decide if you could see yourself doing this work some day. Explain why or why not."

With instructions broken into smaller, action-oriented steps and with emphasis on the present rather than the future as a place to start, Sara would have been more likely to connect with her Sensing students in a way that motivated their mental energy. Susan's response to Sara's original instructions ("What does this have to do with anything real?") suggests Susan's mind may be engaged best through Sensing.

Sara's first words of instruction, which used the word "imagine," would generally be a high motivator for minds that have a preference for Intuition. These minds are engaged both by the endless possibilities implied by this word as well as the assignment's focus on the future ("Imagine yourself as an adult."). José's response ("Cool! I like doing this.") suggests his mind may be engaged best through Intuition.

Sara is faced with a dilemma—which set of instructions should she use, as neither used alone is likely to engage *both* kinds of minds enthusiastically. Since Sara can assume her class is composed of both kinds of minds, one solution is to use both sets of instructions and let the students engage themselves. For example, she could offer her students two ways to complete the assignment by saying the following.

You have a choice for this lesson. You may select one of these two options:

Option 1: Imagine yourself as an adult who is working in a job you love. Then write an essay of no more than 500 words about what your typical day is like and why it is so satisfying.

Option 2: Gather information on at least three jobs people do and choose the one that interests you the most. Then describe in writing, using no more than 500 words, what a typical working day is like for people in that field. Finally, decide if you could see yourself doing this work someday. Explain why or why not.

Both options meet Sara's goal of having students express their individual points of view in writing as well as produce material that can later be critiqued for reader interest, use of language, and grammatical construction.

Extraverted and Introverted Expressions of Sensing and Intuition

Sensing and Intuition can be used in an extraverted or an introverted direction. Sensing in its *extraverted* form gathers concrete information through direct physical experience in the outer environment. Students with this preference enjoy experimenting with, finding, or manipulating tangible objects in order to accomplish a practical purpose. They tend to plunge into an activity quickly, wrapping their minds around the assignment as they go along.

On the other hand, Sensing in its *introverted* form gathers factual information quietly in a step-by-step fashion to structure a solid understanding of purpose and process before taking any overt action. Students with an Introverted Sensing preference may seem slow to become engaged, when in reality they are actively making note of as many details as possible and filing them away in their minds to be retrieved as needed. In a group, they are often the students who sit quietly without speaking while much discussion is under way and then later give the group an accurate and helpful synopsis of the points expressed in the discussion.

Intuition in its *extraverted* form uses hunches and inspirations for seeing endless possibilities for something real in the outer world. These are the students who can visualize a hundred different uses for something like a paper clip, who like to make frequent changes in actual situations, or change the way people are dealing with a situation. Teachers and partners on a project can find themselves feeling frustrated when these students enthusiastically make changes at the last minute as yet one more idea has occurred to them.

Intuition in its *introverted* form uses hunches and inspirations for finding meaning or for delving deeper into the possibilities of an idea. It is the function most closely associated with the unconscious from which the hunches are derived. While they may appear quiet on the outside, students with this kind of mind report an incredible river of ideas flowing through their minds and branching off in many directions—some ideas may even find their way to the cosmos!

Whether in Extraverted or Introverted form, the two Perceiving processes (Sensing and Intuition), involve how a mind informs itself and develops an understanding. What people *do* with their perceptions is determined by what decisions they make based on their perceptions. This decision making involves the next dichotomy of mental functions used in Judging.

Thinking and Feeling: How Judgments Are Made

Jung proposes that there are two mental processes for making rational judgments. He classifies the process as Thinking and Feeling. Again, everyone uses both Thinking and Feeling, the question is which is the *more preferred* function for an individual and thus the function through which that person's mind is most easily engaged.

Thinking Judgment: What Is Most Logical?

The Thinking function as Jung uses the term involves stepping back from the perception and making a decision impersonally, through logic and analysis. The Thinking process looks for objective data in the perception and employs a cause-and-effect kind of reasoning. It takes a linear view that considers logical consequences of the perception. It likes to determine a logical principle that can be applied to any number of situations. Students with Thinking as their naturally preferred Judging function are often attracted to math and science or to the technical aspect or principle involved in a problem. Their minds love to ask, "Why?"

Feeling Judgment: What Is the Impact on People?

Jung calls the opposite process for making judgments Feeling. His use of this term is somewhat misleading, so it is important to remember that Feeling as a judging function is different from emotional feelings. Rather, the preference of Feeling makes decisions based on subjective, person-centered values, particularly those that promote relationships and harmony. This function is keenly interested in the impact of a decision on people—all the individual stakeholders. Given the opportunity, they will likely work to have a group's judgment made by consensus in order to evaluate the decision's potential impact on each person and to promote harmonious relationships among group members. Students with Feeling as their naturally preferred Judging function are often attracted to the humanities or the arts or to aspects of technical subjects affecting the lives of people. Their minds love to ask, "Who?"

Thinking and Feeling in the Classroom

When Bob resigned himself to "another no brainer" upon hearing Sara's instructions, he may not have been stimulated by the assignment because he wanted to know the goal of the assignment and to hear more about its analytical component. Sara would have had a better chance of piquing Bob's interest if she had made it clear to her students that the purpose of the assignment was to refine their writing skills and that their essays would be critiqued, analyzed, and edited. Simply writing about an imagined day in the future without a rationale likely seemed pointless to Bob. The Thinking function seeks to problem solve with a goal or purpose in mind that requires logical analysis to achieve.

José's automatic positive response to Sara's instructions ("Cool! I like doing this") most likely is not only due to his engagement by the word *imagine*, but also by his interest in a topic that is personally oriented ("a job you love"). Sara's choice of words in her assignment connected with both José's preferred Perceiving function of Intuition and his preferred Judging function of Feeling. No wonder he found it "cool" and was motivated to take on the assignment!

Extraverted and Introverted Expressions of Thinking and Feeling

The Thinking function in its *extraverted* form is quick to make decisions and apply them to something in the real world. Students with this preferred way of using Thinking judgment set and adhere to deadlines, tend to take charge of situations, get people organized, and see that projects are completed.

The Thinking function in its *introverted* form is also quick to make decisions but has less inclination to impose them on people or situations directly. Students who more often introvert Thinking typically take one of two approaches. They can appear critical and skeptical when they raise questions to get other people to see their points of view rather than state their view points directly, or they may not give any clues, literally keeping their thoughts to themselves. They are probably the most independent of all the personality types and may be oblivious to the needs and feelings of others in pursuit of this quest to reach the best conclusion possible.

The Feeling function in its *extraverted* form strives for outer harmony. Students who extravert Feeling more often are quick to make their opinions known, like to work with others, and lead groups toward a common goal. They particularly enjoy learning activities that involve human life experience, and they seek a positive relationship with their teacher and peers.

The Feeling function in its *introverted* form strives just as diligently to create and maintain *inner* harmony. While students who more often introvert their Feeling function would like for the outer world to be in agreement with their personal values since this contributes to their inner harmony, they are more willing to "agree to disagree" when others do not go along with those things they care most deeply about. This kind of boundary setting is not as easy for those who mainly extravert their Feeling function.

So to summarize, Jung's and Myers' models of personality types help delineate how people find it easiest and most interesting to inform themselves and develop a perception using Sensing or Intuition (Perception functions), and to delineate which of two ways people prefer to evaluate these perceptions and make a decision—either through the use of Thinking or Feeling (Judgment functions). One sure way to encourage procrastination for most of us is to try to engage our minds through the opposites of our preferences—*unless* we can see how they can be used to serve our preferred mental functions.

The Importance of Both Perception and Judgment for Learning

To achieve the highest performance of mental functioning, and therefore learning, both processes of Perception and Judgment must be used. To short-change either the process of perception or the process of judgment is likely to result in either a judgment made too quickly without much substance behind it or a perception that is never evaluated and carried out so nothing comes of it.

Interestingly, Shawndra's response to Sara's instructions is a good example of how even in the absence of a connection with the teacher, the processes of Perception and Judgment still naturally occur. When Shawndra's mind tuned out Sara's instructions to the assignment, her mind still collected information to form a perception—in this case the physical cues from Susan and Bob that were familiar to her using the Sensing function. Her judgment process concluded that these cues indicated Bob and Susan would give Sara a hard time—a judgment personally determined from her own previous experience. Her Feeling function focused on relationships, and, in this case, the *lack* of harmony.

How much better if teachers take charge of engaging all four mental functions through instruction. To do so assures that all students will develop their perception and judgment in more productive ways.

Judging and Perceiving: Dealing with the Outer World

Isabel Myers added a fourth dichotomy to Jung's personality types. She inferred from Jung's writings that an additional dichotomy exists based on the broader processes of Perceiving and Judging. This dichotomy is enormously helpful in understanding the basic attitude an individual takes when relating to the outer world. The Judging–Perceiving dichotomy indicates if a person more often relates to the outer world through his or her judgment function or through his or her perception function. Myers named her fourth dichotomy, not surprisingly, Judging and Perceiving!

People who prefer relating to the external environment through their Judging function (Thinking or Feeling) want decisions made as timely as possible. They purposefully seek closure and organize their time, projects, and lives in order to bring about closure.

Other people prefer relating to the external environment through their Perceiving function (Sensing or Intuition), focusing more on the process. They want to keep options open as long as possible, leaving time and space for either more specific information (using Sensing) or for the discovery of additional possibilities (using Intuition). They thrive on spontaneity and freedom.

GREAT MINDS

"If you talk to a man in a language he understands, that goes to his head. If you talk to him in his language, that goes to his heart."

NELSON MANDELA (born 1918) The black South African leader fought the racist Apartheid regime and was imprisoned for 27 years. Upon his release, he led the peaceful overthrow of Apartheid and guided the country to a transition under a democratic system.

Judging and Perceiving in the Classroom

Students with a preference for Judging tend to begin early working on projects or assignments, complete their work, and turn it in on time. Sometimes, once they make a judgment about an issue, they find it difficult to reopen their minds to other options. However, they often do find it easier to be flexible and open minded when certain structures are in place first—a goal, deadline, or plan.

Students with a preference for perceiving seem more easygoing about assignments and may not show evidence of any work until the last minute. As these students gradually learn the importance of due dates they develop their own sense of timing in order to meet these commitments. Quite often, however, students with a preference for Perceiving may clash with the Judging preference held by most (but not all) teachers and educational administrators who want reassurance early in a process that a due date will be met.

From Preferences to Personality Types

You now have the basics of personality type. The four mental functions of Sensing, Intuition, Thinking, and Feeling are all equally valuable and important. We all use each of them at different times in different circumstances and in both an extraverted and introverted direction. However, with each of these dichotomies, most of us have been inclined through brain hardwiring and environmental influence to develop a more natural preference for one of each of the pairs. It is through this natural preference that our minds are most easily engaged. From use of this natural preference first, we can more easily intentionally take the second step of including the use of the opposite preference. Thus we arrive at a more complete perception or a wiser judgment.

Using the four dichotomies, we see that there are sixteen possible combinations of preferences. These sixteen combinations form the sixteen different personality types. These sixteen whole types more accurately reflect how we each experience our preferences as indicated in the following table of the types. In this table you will notice the use of initials to identify the types with the letter *N* for Intuition in place of an *I* already used for Introversion. Myers suggested this convention of initials because the words for the preferences have so many interpretations associated with them. Therefore, dichotomies in this shorthand form become:

The type table is a very useful tool to which we will refer throughout this book. It is also important to recognize that personality type is not static and that people differ within each type. Jung's theory of personality types is a developmental one, the characteristics of which we discuss in more depth in chapter 5. Psychologist Susan Brock[1] suggested one's type is rather like a zip code: there are many different neighborhoods, streets, and house numbers in an address, but the zip code does indicate a basic guideline for where a person lives. Myers herself said, "Every ENFP is like every other ENFP, is like some other ENFPs, is like no other ENFP."[2] *How* a type is expressed is influenced by countless other factors.

Figure 1.2 *Type Table*

ISTJ

For ISTJs the dominant quality in their lives is an abiding sense of responsibility for doing what needs to be done in the here-and-now. Their realism, organizing abilities, and command of the facts lead to the thorough completion of tasks and with great attention to detail. Logical pragmatists at heart, ISTJs make decisions based on their experience and with an eye to efficiency in all things. ISTJs are intensely committed to people and to the organizations of which they are a part; they take their work seriously and believe others should do so as well.

ISTP

For ISTPs the driving force in their lives is to understand how things and phenomena in the real world work so they can make the best and most effective use of them. They are logical and realistic people, and they are natural troubleshooters. When not actively solving a problem, ISTPs are quiet and analytical observers of their environment, and they naturally look for the underlying sense to any facts they have gathered. ISTPs often pursue variety and even excitement in their hands-on experiences. Although they do have a spontaneous, even playful side, what people often first encounter with them is their detached pragmatism.

ESTP

For ESTPs the dominant quality in their lives is their enthusiastic attention to the outer world of hands-on and real-life experiences. ESTPs are excited by continuous involvement in new activities and in the pursuit of new challenges. They tend to be logical and analytical in their approach to life, and they have an acute sense of how objects, events, and people in the world work. ESTPs are typically energetic and adaptable realists, who prefer to experience and accept life rather than to judge or organize it.

ESTJ

For ESTJs the driving force in their lives is their need to analyze and bring into logical order the outer world of events, people, and things. ESTJs like to organize anything that comes into their domain, and they will work energetically to complete tasks so they can quickly move from one to the next. Sensing orients their thinking to current facts and realities, and thus gives their thinking a pragmatic quality. ESTJs take their responsibilities seriously and believe others should do so as well.

ISFJ

For ISFJs the dominant quality in their lives is an abiding respect and sense of personal responsibility for doing what needs to be done in the here-and-now. Actions that are of practical help to others are of particular importance to ISFJs. Their realism, organizing abilities, and command of the facts lead to their thorough attention in completing tasks. ISFJs bring an aura of quiet warmth, caring, and dependability to all that they do; they take their work seriously and believe others should do so as well.

ISFP

For ISFPs the dominant quality in their lives is a deep-felt caring for living things, combined with a quietly playful and sometimes adventurous approach to life and all its experiences. ISFPs typically show their caring in very practical ways, since they often prefer action to words. Their warmth and concern are generally not expressed openly, and what people often first encounter with ISFPs is their quiet adaptability, realism, and "free spirit" spontaneity.

ESFP

For ESFPs the dominant quality in their lives is their enthusiastic attention to the outer world of hands-on and real-life experiences. ESFPs are excited by continuous involvement in new activities and new relationships. They also have a deep concern for people, and they show their caring in warm and pragmatic gestures of helping. ESFPs are typically energetic and adaptable realists, who prefer to experience and accept life rather than to judge or organize it.

ESFJ

For ESFJs the dominant quality in their lives is an active and intense caring about people and a strong desire to bring harmony into their relationships. ESFJs bring an aura of warmth to all that they do, and they naturally move into action to help others, to organize the world around them, and to get things done. Sensing orients their feeling to current facts and realities, and thus gives their feeling a hands-on pragmatic quality. ESFJs take their work seriously and believe others should do so as well.

Figure 1.2 *Type Table continued*

INFJ

For INFJs the dominant quality in their lives is their attention to the inner world of possibilities, ideas, and symbols. Knowing by way of insight is paramount for them, and they often manifest a deep concern for people and relationships as well. INFJs often have deep interests in creative expression as well as issues of spirituality and human development. While their energy and attention are naturally drawn to the inner world of ideas and insights, what people often first encounter with INFJs is their drive for closure and for the application of their ideas to people's concerns.

INFP

For INFPs the dominant quality in their lives is a deep-felt caring and idealism about people. They experience this intense caring most often in their relationships with others, but they may also experience it around ideas, projects, or any involvement they see as important. INFPs are often skilled communicators, and they are naturally drawn to ideas that embody a concern for human potential. INFPs live in the inner world of values and ideals, but what people often first encounter with them in the outer world is their adaptability and concern for possibilities.

ENFP

For ENFPs the dominant quality in their lives is their attention to the outer world of possibilities; they are excited by continuous involvement in anything new, whether it be new ideas, new people, or new activities. Though ENFPs thrive on what is possible and what is new, they experience a deep concern for people as well. Thus, they are especially interested in possibilities for people. ENFPs are typically energetic, enthusiastic people who lead spontaneous and adaptable lives.

ENFJ

For ENFJs the dominant quality in their lives is an active and intense caring about people and a strong desire to bring harmony into their relationships. ENFJs are openly expressive and empathic people who bring an aura of warmth to all that they do. Intuition orients their feeling to the new and to the possible, thus they often enjoy working to manifest a humanitarian vision, or helping others develop their potential. ENFJs naturally and conscientiously move into action to care for others, to organize the world around them, and to get things done.

INTJ

For INTJs the dominant force in their lives is their attention to the inner world of possibilities, symbols, abstractions, images, and thoughts. Insight in conjunction with logical analysis is the essence of their approach to the world; they think systemically. Ideas are the substance of life for INTJs and they have a driving need to understand, to know, and to demonstrate competence in their areas of interest. INTJs inherently trust their insights, and with their task-orientation will work intensely to make their visions into realities.

INTP

For INTPs the driving force in their lives is to understand whatever phenomenon is the focus of their attention. They want to make sense of the world—as a concept—and they often enjoy opportunities to be creative. INTPs are logical, analytical, and detached in their approach to the world; they naturally question and critique ideas and events as they strive for understanding. INTPs usually have little need to control the outer world, or to bring order to it, and they often appear very flexible and adaptable in their lifestyle.

ENTP

For ENTPs the dominant quality in their lives is their attention to the outer world of possibilities; they are excited by continuous involvement in anything new, whether it be new ideas, new people, or new activities. They look for patterns and meaning in the world, and they often have a deep need to analyze, to understand, and to know the nature of things. ENTPs are typically energetic, enthusiastic people who lead spontaneous and adaptable lives.

ENTJ

For ENTJs the driving force in their lives is their need to analyze and bring into logical order the outer world of events, people, and things. ENTJs are natural leaders who build conceptual models that serve as plans for strategic action. Intuition orients their thinking to the future, and gives their thinking an abstract quality. ENTJs will actively pursue and direct others in the pursuit of goals they have set, and they prefer a world that is structured and organized.

Think of each of these sixteen types as sixteen possible gateways to engaging a mind. And before you flinch at the prospect of providing sixteen different ways for each lesson to be learned, be assured that no one in her right mind would recommend that! However, we would like you to entertain the possibility that there may be up to sixteen types represented in your classroom and that there are ways to engage each of them without losing your sanity!

And while these opposite mental functions and attitudes may not roll off your tongue just yet, read on to understand better how the use of personality types can transform your classroom and your school.

In a Nutshell

- A teacher's task is to engage each student personally in the learning process.
- One way to connect and engage students is through the intentional use of personality type.
- Jung's personality types involve four dichotomies used by our minds, each pole of which is equally valuable and important.
- Two opposite directions and sources of mental energy are Extraversion and Introversion.
- Two opposite ways of forming perceptions are Sensing and Intuition.
- Two opposite ways of making judgments are Thinking and Feeling.
- Two opposite ways of connecting with the world outside ourselves are Judging and Perceiving.
- People have a natural preference for one pole on each of the four dichotomies.
- Students are more highly motivated when their natural preferences are engaged, and they are more likely to be disengaged when their natural preferences are ignored.

Check Your Understanding

Q *What is the key difference between Extraversion and Introversion?*
A The source of energy is different for Extraverts and Introverts. Extraverts get their energy from the environment outside themselves. Introverts get their energy from within themselves. Extraverts are energized by the world of action and interaction. Introverts are energized by their inner world of reflection and ideas.

SCENARIO: *Alice came to school early because she wanted some quiet time before her colleagues and the students arrived. After some time alone she was ready to discuss the newest teaching strategy with other teachers and interact with her students.*

Q *Is Alice's behavior more likely an example of Extraversion or Introversion?*

A Introversion. Introverts whose work requires a good deal of extraversion often like to charge their mental energy with a period of quiet reflection at the beginning of the day.

SCENARIO: *John was tired when he arrived at school in the morning but after he had talked to a few colleagues and several students he began to feel energized. He was no longer tired and couldn't wait to begin teaching his first period class!*

Q *Is John's behavior more likely an example of Extraversion or Introversion?*

A Extraversion. Engagement with the outer world is the direction and source of energy for Extraverts, and John likely recharges his energy through interaction with the world around him.

Q *What is the critical difference between the Perceiving functions of Sensing and Intuition?*

A Sensing looks for specific, discrete, verifiable information and gives order to this information for realistic, practical purposes. Intuition looks for meaning from hunches, insights, and relationships and applies this to a big-picture perspective and future possibilities.

SCENARIO: *Barry could walk into his classroom and quickly notice if there was anything new on the bulletin board, if his friend Chad had on a new pair of jeans, or if there were fewer chairs in the room than usual. His teacher also noticed that Barry learned to read new words more easily if he could hear them pronounced phonetically.*

Q *Is Barry's perceiving more an example of Sensing or Intuition?*

A Sensing, as that is the function that likes to focus on specifics and to sort something complex into its smaller pieces.

SCENARIO: *Theresa loves to read and enjoys books that make almost poetic use of words. She isn't always sure of what some of the new words mean, but she is satisfied to get the general gist of their meaning from the context in which they are written. With her own writing, she often receives high marks for her ideas but some of her teachers ask her to support these ideas with data, a request that is frustrating to her. She believes her ideas and creativity ought to stand on their own merit.*

Q *Is Theresa's use of language more an example of Sensing or Intuition?*

A Intuition, which is more interested in "meaning" than in specific data points and which typically finds meaning from larger contexts.

Q *What is the critical difference between the Judging functions of Thinking and Feeling?*

A The Thinking function makes rational decisions based on logical analysis of objective data. The Feeling function makes rational decisions based on person-centered values that promote harmony.

SCENARIO: *Janet is the lead teacher of a middle school teaching team that is charged with determining where a mandated 10 percent cut can be made in the budget for her grade level. The time frame is short, making it difficult to call a meeting, and she decides to cut each teacher's budget by 10 percent in order to make a fair and efficient decision.*

Q *Is Janet's approach more indicative of the Thinking or the Feeling function?*

A Most likely Thinking. The Thinking function seeks objective data that can be analyzed for a logical conclusion and one that can be applied equitably if fairness is an issue.

SCENARIO: *Dave is the lead teacher of another middle school team that is charged with the identical mandate of a 10 percent cut in its budget with the same short time limit. Dave knows time is short so he immediately asks his team members to look at their individual expenses and be prepared to attend a meeting after school the next day to work together to determine where cuts can be made.*

Q *Is Dave's behavior more indicative of the Thinking or the Feeling function?*

A Most likely Feeling. The Feeling function likes to take individual circumstances into account in making decisions in order to be fair and to promote harmony. Those with a preference for Feeling also like to make decisions through consensus.

Q *What is the critical difference between the Judging attitude and the Perceiving attitude toward the outer world?*

A People who prefer relating to the external world through their Judging function seek closure and organize their time, projects, and lives with a view toward closure. People who prefer relating to the external world through their Perceiving function typically want to keep their options open as long as possible and focus on process. They usually thrive on flexibility and spontaneity.

SCENARIO: *Jennifer completed reading the required three short stories for her English class, and prepared her summary of each story and the analysis of the similarities and differences between the main characters in the stories. She turned in her paper two days before the due date.*

Q *Is Jennifer's behavior more typical for the Judging or the Perceiving attitude?*

A Judging, because she approached the assignment in a structured fashion and completed it well before the deadline.

SCENARIO: *Anna delayed beginning her reading of the required short stories until the night before the assignment was due. She had been invited to attend several parties over the weekend and then some of her friends asked her to go with them to the soccer game. It was a big game, and she didn't want to miss it! When she got home, her mother reminded her that she had promised to call her favorite aunt and Anna had a lot of news to share. Anna didn't start reading the short stories until almost 10 p.m. She stayed up late, and then got up an hour before her usual time to finish the assignment.*

Q *Is Anna's behavior more an example of the Judging or Perceiving attitude?*

A Perceiving. Anna focused on living each moment to the fullest and was energized at the last moment against a deadline to complete her assignment.

- Think about your own preferences and come up with several examples to illustrate them.

- Discuss with a family member, friend, or a colleague your typical way of going about a new task. Explore how your behavior might be related to your type preferences.

2

Personalizing Instruction

*Some price, modest or substantial, must be paid any
time a mind is forced or attempts to learn or perform
something in a way for which it is not wired.*

MEL LEVINE, *A Mind at a Time*

Research shows that personalized learning can increase attendance,
decrease dropout rates, and decrease disruptive behavior."[1] Yet needless to say, a
teacher with twenty-five students (or more!) in a classroom that may include
sixteen different personality types cannot provide sixteen different ways of meeting
a particular learning objective. Even if it were possible, it would not be recommended. Students need to use their entire minds—not just their preferences. So
how does the teacher *engage* all sixteen kinds of minds through their natural preferences in order for those minds to learn in a way that is most effective?

Although each of the sixteen types has its own dynamics and unique learning
pattern, for practical purposes of general lesson design, compressing the sixteen
combinations into groupings of the preferences provides effective categories for
working with basic learning differences. Because we focus in this book on the core
mental processes of perception and judgment, we will most often use a grouping
referred to as "function pairs," which are four combinations of Sensing and
Intuition with Thinking and Feeling:[2]

Sensing with Thinking (ST)
Sensing with Feeling (SF)
Intuition with Feeling (NF)
Intuition with Thinking (NT)

While the four types that fall within each of these function pairs have some
major differences, there is much that they hold in common.

ST Types (ESTJ, ESTP, ISTJ, ISTP)

ST types focus on efficient accomplishment of tasks by combining the specificity and practicality of Sensing with the logical and analytical evaluation of Thinking.

SF Types (ESFJ, ESFP, ISFJ, ISFP)

SF types focus on meeting the practical needs of people in their everyday lives by combining the specificity and practicality of Sensing with the person-centered evaluation process of Feeling.

NF Types (ENFJ, ENFP, INFJ, INFP)

NF types focus on human growth and development by combining the global, future-possibility perspective of Intuition with the person-centered evaluation process of Feeling.

NT Types (ENTJ, ENTP, INTJ, INTP)

NT types focus on analytical problem solving by combining the global, future-possibility perspective of Intuition with the logical, analytical evaluation of Thinking.

With time and experience, teachers can amplify these groupings, planning for the important mental energy sources of Extraversion and Introversion and the preferred way of interacting with the outer world with either Judging or Perceiving. However, the use of simpler groupings is a practical way for personalizing some fundamental aspects of instruction.

In this section, we will focus on applications related to three areas: (1) the words used by the teacher, (2) selection of learning strategies, and (3) improving student time management and work habits.

Personalize Words of Instruction

As was demonstrated in chapter 1, the very words a teacher uses to introduce a lesson or give directions for a learning activity are likely to motivate some types while turning off others, even if the topic or objective itself might have some appeal. This is particularly true of verbs. The practical and pragmatic Sensing and Thinking (ST) types respond more positively to words like "make" or "apply" than to the less-definitive words like "imagine," or "create." The naturally collaborative Sensing and Feeling (SF) types report more motivation with words like "express," or "share" than words like "analyze" or "dictate." The independent and personalizing Intuition and Feeling (NF) types respond with more energy to the words "elaborate" or "fantasize," than to the words "memorize" or "list." And the analytical, problem-solving Intuition and Thinking (NT) types are motivated by words such as "solve" or "critique" rather than by words such as "specify" or "copy."

We went directly to the types and asked for examples of words that either motivate them or lead to disinterest and likely disengagement (tables 2.a and 2.b). See which list has the most words that motivate you, note the preferences involved, and then check the list associated with the opposite preferences. Do you notice any difference in your own response to these verbs?

Engaging Words

Given the choice, would you be more engaged as a student if the teacher used the list that coincides with your preferences rather than that of the opposite preferences? If you as an adult recognize a difference in your response to these words fairly easily, then most likely you can understand their impact on students in a classroom.

Table 2.a *Engaging Words*

Sensing and Thinking (ST)	Sensing and Feeling (SF)	Intuition and Feeling (NF)	Intuition and Thinking (NT)
Make	Express	Elaborate	Solve
Apply	Share	Fantasize	Critique
Assemble	Show	Dream	Develop
See	Make	Create	Write
Name	Discuss	Pretend	Create
Design	Explain	Design	Debate
Show	Name	Discover	Design
Build	Cooperate	Build	Discover
Order	Visit	Explore	Collaborate
Touch	Touch	Make	Generate
Act	Help	Discuss	Experiment
Depict	Watch	Clarify	Consider
Watch	Tell	Tell	Explore
Examine	Describe	Imagine	Find a new …
Observe	Contribute	Change	Synthesize
Suggest	Work with someone and …	Debate	Examine
Mix		Brainstorm	Compute
Experience	Choose	Envision	Illustrate
Investigate	Give	Generate	Determine
Indicate	Request	Paraphrase	Analyze
Simplify	Enjoy	Reform	Edit
Find	Meet	Show	Systematize
Use	Put together	Solve	Categorize
Fix	Assist	Request	Figure out
Notice	Suggest	Enjoy	Find a pattern
Take	Provide	Experiment	Produce

Table 2.b *Disengaging Words*

Sensing and Thinking (ST)	Sensing and Feeling (SF)	Intuition and Feeling (NF)	Intuition and Thinking (NT)
Imagine	Analyze	Memorize	Specify
Create	Dictate	List	Copy
Pretend	Theorize	Compute	Explain
Recite	Classify	Spell	List
Debate	Recite	Outline	Practice
Relate	Expound	Apply	Label
Discuss	Create	Practice	Detail
Design	Design	Recall	Repeat
Describe	Imagine	Specify	Imitate
Share	Categorize	Limit	Report
Theorize	Memorize	Prioritize	Fill in
Memorize	Compete	Sequence	Review
Visualize	Visualize	Find the facts	Memorize
Expound	Contemplate	Examine	Duplicate
Contemplate	Speculate	Narrow down	Reassess
Dictate	Investigate	Detail	Follow

RESOURCES

RESOURCE 2, *Learning Preferences by Type: Words and Activities that Work,* provides a list of these words that can be kept handy as a reference sheet when preparing instructions.

Personalize Learning Activities

One of the most powerful options available to teachers to increase student engagement is personal choice. *Internal* motivation is strongest when stimulated by choice, not by command. This opportunity for choice is a major element of what makes us human. Once we make a choice, we claim responsibility for the outcome; something now matters to us and we take the steps necessary to see that it comes about. By providing this external stimulus of choice, the teacher places the responsibility on the student to implement the choice or perhaps to make the choice not to act at all. Either way, the student is in charge of his or her own behavior and develops the life skill of responsible decision making required in the adult world. Two areas where choice may be critical to student achievement are learning activities and assessment of learning.

Let's look first at choice of learning activities; for again, what motivates one personality type is often a turnoff to another. A beneficial consequence of giving students choices is that learning becomes more personalized for them and hence increases the likelihood of student engagement. We asked students who represented the types to tell us what learning activities motivated them to be interested in a topic or assignment (table 2.c). Note these differences in learning activities reported by the types as *engaging*.

Table 2.c *Engaging Learning Activities*

Sensing and Thinking (ST)	Sensing and Feeling (SF)	Intuition and Feeling (NF)	Intuition and Thinking (NT)
Competitions	Show & Tell	Noncompetitive games	Self-instruction
Demonstrations	Peer tutoring	Simulations	Research & reporting
Field trips	Cooperative learning	Group activities	Games of strategy
Physical projects	Small group projects	Seminar discussions of personal or social issues	Designing & carrying out experiments
Re-enactments	Personal sharing	Role-play	Debates
Collecting things	Giving reports	Arts projects	Simulations
Laboratory experiments	Art activities	Drama	Brain teasers
Videos	Videos	Cooperative learning	Seminars
Interactive computer	Simulations	Field trips	Designing graphs
	Reading about people	Lab experiments	Needs assessments
		Writing about something one can identify with personally	Discovery labs
		Fantasizing	Individual programmed learning
		Reward system	Creative writing
			Lectures by experts
			Complex word problems

A close examination of the lists reveals patterns and generalities. The Sensing–Thinking types, who like to deal with factual or manual skills, emphasize physical activities and working with inanimate objects or data. The Sensing–Feeling types, who tend to focus on factual realities related to people, emphasize activities that involve interaction and sharing. The Intuitive–Feeling types, who like to deal with possibilities and human development, report engagement with interpersonal and intrapersonal expression as most motivating. The Intuitive-Thinking types, who are natural analytical problem solvers, emphasize intellectual activity and independent learning. The Intuitive types list more activities, perhaps reflecting the breadth of possibilities that interests the Intuitive function.

Just as important to know are the activities the students of different types report as leading to *dis*engagement (table 2.d):

Table 2.d *Disengaging Learning Activities*

Sensing and Thinking (ST)	Sensing and Feeling (SF)	Intuition and Feeling (NF)	Intuition and Thinking (NT)
Brainstorming	Research	Worksheets	Role-play
Research	Brainstorming	True/false questions	Guided practice
Writing essays	Debates	Drill & repetition	Drill & repetition
Fantasizing	Lectures	Making outlines	Worksheets
Role-play	Writing essays	Competitive games where someone loses	Sharing feelings
Debates	Competitive games		Games which don't require strategizing
Fictional stories	Games of strategy		Anything which has only one answer
Open-ended discussions			

GREAT MINDS

"Whoever controls the education of our children controls our future."

WILMA PEARL MANKILLER (born 1945) When this Oklahoma native rose to principal chief of the Cherokee nation in 1985, she became the first female leader of a Native American tribe. She worked tirelessly for the growth and development of the Cherokee nation and for rights, education, and equal opportunities for Native American people.

Some activities engage students across the types—for example field trips and laboratory experiments. But as the principles of personality type suggest, some kinds of activities that engage one type clearly do not engage others. Note some of these differences if we compare opposite types (table 2.e).

Table 2.e *Learning Activities: Opposite Types*

Sensing and Thinking (ST)	Intuition and Feeling (NF)	Intuition and Thinking (NT)	Sensing and Feeling (SF)
Engaging: Competition	*Disengaging:* Competitive games where someone loses	*Engaging:* Research and reporting	*Disengaging:* Research
Disengaging: Open-ended Discussions	*Engaging:* Seminar discussions of personal or social issues	*Disengaging:* Sharing feelings *Engaging:* Debates	*Engaging:* Personal sharing *Disengaging:* Debates
Disengaging: Role-play	*Engaging:* Role-play	*Engaging:* Independent Learning activities and self-instruction	*Engaging:* Peer tutoring and cooperative learning

Does this mean that teachers always need to offer four choices for how lessons are to be learned? Certainly not! Yet what these differences do suggest is that to engage each student each day, a teacher needs to vary learning activities throughout the day, being informed and alert enough to appeal to the four type groupings as equally as possible. And fairly frequently, teachers should offer students choices for how they will learn a particular lesson, basing the choices on differences among the type groupings—even four choices when possible.

Interestingly, when asked the question, "What engages you and what disengages you to learn?" few students included reading in either category. Yet reading is one of the most important skills needed for success in school. This is an area where choice of material to be read can make a significant difference in motivation. The differences outlined in the following table suggest the wisdom of providing and allowing students to select from a variety of reading sources. As you can see, given a choice, students of different types tend to select different materials to read.

Sensing–Thinking (ST)

Technical material; adventure stories; information about their hobbies

Sensing–Feeling (SF)

Biographies; stories about people dealing with daily issues

Intuition–Feeling (NF)

Fantasy; books with an artistic, psychological, or spiritual bent; fiction about relationships; poetry

Intuition–Thinking (NT)

Books with complex plots; mysteries; fiction that increases a knowledge base; science fiction

By using personality types as the foundation for developing learning activities, teachers ensure there is an appropriate balance in the use of perception and judgment by students since each activity will include both processes. This approach ensures the engagement of the widely differing minds in the classroom. Just as important, these learning choices visibly affirm the differences among the minds as equally good. And to the extent a particular learning activity requires collaborative work, students observe that different strengths are needed and can be appreciated, and thus they learn to welcome all kinds of minds on the team. Self-concepts thrive and achievement increases.

Example of Lesson Design

Let's assume Sara, the teacher of José, Susan, Bob, and Shawndra, wants to maximize engagement of her students in a lesson focused on writing effectively about a personal point of view. She elects to offer four approaches to the assignment. A step-by-step example of how she could use type knowledge in designing her lesson might go like this.

1. **Sara begins with a learning objective from the curriculum.**
   In this case, the goal is for students to be able to write effectively about a personal point of view so that it is interesting to others, uses appropriate language and paragraph structure, and is grammatically correct.

2. **Next, Sara develops an introductory activity** to get students' attention, explain the objective, and help students give personal relevance to the learning. The activity provides a context in which the learning takes place and gives students a reason for the learning. It is also an opportunity to demonstrate or give an example.

Sara shows a video of adults working in a variety of careers. She asks students to identify and write down the jobs that interest them the most or indicate if they found none of these jobs interesting.

She then tells her students that while some things don't necessarily have to be expressed in words, there are some things we decide that are so important that we need to use words in order for others to understand them clearly. And while oral explanations sometimes work, there are other situations where we need to be able to *write* our viewpoints in clear and interesting ways so that other people can understand what we want to express.

Sara might give students examples such as writing a letter to apply for a job, or writing an e-mail to a friend in another city about why you've decided to attend a particular college. At this point, Sara could show them an example of a well-written letter soliciting a job, highlighting effective use of sentence structure, grammar, and appeal to reader interest. She might also want to show students a letter written poorly that might prevent them from getting the job.

3. **To introduce the assignment, Sara then asks her students to think** for a few minutes about the reasons that may have caused them to be interested (or not interested) in the jobs they selected and to jot down a few words that explain one or more of these reasons. After asking for a few examples to be shared, Sara then tells her students that the goal of the lesson is to use effectively written words to express their thoughts in a way that other people can understand their point of view. She reminds them to use appropriate language and paragraph structure as well as correct grammar.

She tells her students they will have four choices for the assignment. She asks them to select one of the choices and gives them the dates that their first drafts and the completed assignments are due. She also lets her students know that if they have another idea for an assignment that would meet the same objective, they may propose that to her—preferably in writing with an explanation of why it is a good alternative for their learning.

The following are the choices of assignments for each of the four type groups of ST, SF, NF, and NT: (The material presented to the students would not be labeled by type preferences.)

Choice 1. Sensing and Thinking (ST)
(Often motivated by defined tasks)

- Find information on three jobs people do.
- Choose a job that interests you the most.
- Write a description, using no more than 500 words, of what a typical work day is like for people in that field.
- Decide if you could see yourself doing this work some day. Explain why or why not.

Choice 2. Sensing and Feeling (SF)
(Often motivated by day-to-day specifics of the lives of people they can connect with)

- Either on your own, or with a friend, ask three adults to describe the work they do each day.
- Reflect on your own or discuss with your friend what you've learned from the discussions.
- Choose the line of work that interests you the most.
- Decide if you could see yourself doing this work some day.
- Write a description of what you learned and explain why you would (or would not) like to do this work yourself. Use no more than 500 words.

Choice 3. Intuition and Feeling (NF)
(Often motivated by open-ended options they can relate to personally)

Imagine yourself as an adult who is working in a job you love. This can be work you already know about, a job you are interested in, or perhaps something no one else has ever done. Describe in writing, using up to 500 words, what a typical working day is like for people in that field and why you would find this work very satisfying.

Choice 4. Intuition and Thinking (NT)
(Often motivated by forming opinions on large issues)

> Put yourself in the role of a journalist writing for the career section of a newspaper. The assignment given by your editor is to research and report on career fields that look promising for young people, including at least one you would find interesting to engage in yourself. Write a column on one or more careers you find that fit these criteria, explaining why they are promising and why at least one is interesting to you. Column space is limited by the paper to a 500-word maximum.

4. **Sara reminds her students of the core grammatical skills** they learned previously and refers them to a "checklist" she has posted. She tells her students she will be available to answer questions and help anyone who needs her assistance.

5. **When the first drafts are brought to class,** Sara gives her students a set of guidelines that provide the criteria against which their writing will be measured and asks them to begin editing as needed. As students work independently, she circulates among students and notices their level of understanding and use of basic writing skills at the same time she is coaching and assisting.

6. **After the students have edited and revised their material independently,** Sara may have them share their papers with a peer in class for editing and for gauging the level of reader interest and clarity of expression. The peer editors could evaluate the paper using the guidelines the teacher developed for grammatical principles as well—an opportunity to repeat a learning process, only this time in the role of an "expert." As the most skilled expert, of course, Sara will also want to read and grade the student papers herself following the self-assessment and peer editing.

GREAT MINDS

"All my life I have tried to pluck a thistle and plant a flower wherever the flower would grow in thought and mind."

ABRAHAM LINCOLN (1809–1865) The sixteenth president of the United States led the Union during the Civil War and defeated the Confederacy, in the process unifying the country, freeing blacks from slavery, and enshrining in the Constitution the idea that Americans are equal under the law, no matter their race.

Even when given choices, Sara's students may not always select assignments that match their type preferences. They may select assignments based on their levels of interest in the topic, accessibility of resources, or choices made by friends with whom they'd like to work. Yet whether they do or do not select a type match, it is still a winning proposition. The dynamic of choice alone usually creates engagement and positive momentum, and over time students will exercise and develop all their mental functions to some extent.

Research on selection of school subjects, college majors, and careers shows clearly that given enough leeway, people gravitate toward those activities that allow them to use and develop their natural preferences for perception (Sensing or Intuition) and judgment (Thinking or Feeling). These people also report the greatest sense of satisfaction. Providing an environment for these kinds of choices in the school environment makes achievement more likely and fosters a greater sense of competency and satisfaction as a natural component of life.

RESOURCES

RESOURCE 6, *Engaging Students of All Types*, for incorporating the preferences into lesson design. RESOURCE 7, *Sample Lessons for Introducing Type*, for examples of lessons.

Direct Instruction and Type

The term "direct instruction" as a teaching strategy means different things to different educators. To some it equates to a lecture by the teacher. To others it is a teacher-directed, step-by-step approach to teaching a lesson, usually involving a lecture related to a specific objective and standard of achievement. In addition, strategies may include teacher demonstrations, supervised practice and application, ongoing checks for students' understanding by the teacher, and evaluation of learning. While used initially as a very structured, fast-paced, scripted method of instruction, the term *direct instruction* now is often used more generically.

What is common to the various interpretations of direct instruction, as with all forms of instruction, is that the teacher is in charge of clearly stated objectives and established standards against which student performance is measured on a continual basis. In addition, direct presentation is used as one of the teaching strategies—particularly for giving the lesson relevance to students and for the teaching of core knowledge and basic skills. Building on these skills occurs in a planned, incremental fashion.

The integration of type enhances direct instruction, as well as other approaches to teaching and learning. Introduction of the topic, learning objectives, lectures, and other learning activities can all contribute to personalizing the learning if the teacher includes concrete elements for the Sensing preference, conceptual material for Intuition, a purpose that is logical for Thinking, and a purpose that is personally beneficial to individuals for Feeling. One might call these "mind breaks" that can be every bit as rejuvenating as a food break at an educational conference!

Sara's stated curriculum objective is "Students will be able to write effectively about a personal point of view so that it is interesting to others, uses appropriate language and paragraph structure, and is grammatically correct." Sara selected an introductory activity concerning jobs to allow her to get her students' attention across types and then cleverly elicits other suggestions from her students for when effective writing is needed—purposes that *they* find engaging. Up her sleeve, of course, are a few purposes she can contribute as well:

- To write a letter to get a job (ST)
- To write a story (SF)
- To write a letter to a friend giving reasons why you think he or she is making a mistake about something (NF)
- To influence a group of people to accept your viewpoint (NT)

Following are three other examples of areas of direct instruction where a teacher can intentionally involve type for motivating and engaging students.

1. **Teacher Presentation**
   - **Support abstract concepts (Intuition) with concrete examples (Sensing).**

     Globalization is a reality that cannot be escaped in today's technological environment and can be used for good or evil (Intuition). For example, technology has made useful information exchange available worldwide. At the same time, technology has made communication between terrorist groups in different countries easier (Sensing).

   - **When basic and essential information is the focus of the presentation (Sensing), the teacher should also tell students early on about some possibilities for future uses (Intuition).**

     Today's lesson will be about learning how to use the materials safely in (a particular science lab experiment). Later, we'll focus on the implications (of this particular experiment) for improving people's lives and solving some of the world's problems.

- Apply core knowledge and examples to general principles (engages Thinking) and relate core knowledge and examples to a person (engages Feeling).

If teaching the new vocabulary word "intrusive" and illustrating its use in a sentence the teacher might give the following two examples: "When the school board initiated a dress code, many students believed its policy was too intrusive on the students' personal rights" (Thinking); and also "Maria considered Steve intrusive when he asked to see her journal entry" (Feeling).

2. **"Wait Time" After Teacher Asks Probing Questions**
   - Eliminates competition for "air time" and levels the playing field for Introverts who give their best answer after reflection.

   - Helps Extraverts access and develop their introverted side for thoughtful answers when discussion isn't an option.

3. **Talk It Over in Pairs Before Answering Probing Questions**
   - Allows Extraverts to talk their way to an answer.

   - Allows Introverts to access and develop their extraverted side and learn to risk speaking their initial thoughts sooner when it is expedient to do so.

v v v v v
^ ^ ^ ^ ^

The important principle here is to develop sufficient awareness of how minds are engaged differently by type and to begin intentionally to incorporate this awareness into teacher-directed instruction where the teacher has most control. If type is new for the teacher, then the same principles apply as they do for student learning.

1) Begin with what you already know (e.g., some ways students learn differently).

2) Incrementally build on this knowledge with the introduction of new concepts and behaviors (e.g., evaluating an established lesson for accommodation of Extraversion and Introversion and adapting the lesson if needed to accommodate both).

3) Assess the effect of what you've tried.

4) Based on this evaluation add an additional type accommodation (e.g., directions that engage both Sensing and Intuition).

5) Assess the result of this addition.

Engaging Students of All Types

A useful tool to increase knowledge and awareness while beginning to design lessons based on type is a set of questions that serves as a "self-check list." With time and practice, questions such as the following become automatic.

Extraversion

○ Have you included opportunities for students to interact with other students and the teacher?

○ Have you included opportunities for students to talk about the concepts, information, issues, and ideas with others?

○ Have you included opportunities for student movement?

Introversion

○ Have you included opportunities for students to reflect and process the information presented in the lesson?

○ Have you included opportunities for students to work independently?

○ Have students who like to process a question before answering it orally had opportunities to do so?

○ Have you given students the choice to present assignments in either written or oral form?

Sensing

○ Have you included an outline or overview of the structure of the lesson?

○ Have you included a practical purpose for the lesson?

○ Is the lesson presented in a systematic manner with step-by-step instructions?

○ Have you included concrete examples?

○ Are sufficient facts and details included?

○ Are expectations for students clear and easily understood?

○ Are directions for activities and assignments clear and concise?

○ Does the lesson include practical and useful applications?

○ Are classroom procedures established and known by students?

Intuition

○ Have you provided students with the "big picture" of what they are to learn?

○ Have you included concepts and possibilities, patterns and relationships in your presentation?

○ Are there opportunities for students to be creative, original, and imaginative?

○ Have you included a variety of activities?

○ Are students allowed to work at their own pace in order to meet the given deadline for completion?

Thinking

○ Is there a logical purpose given for the lesson?

○ Have you included opportunities for students to analyze and synthesize?

○ Do you allow students to discuss and debate issues?

○ Are you comfortable when students question or challenge you, or ask, "why?"

○ Do you include assignments that allow students to use logical analysis, experiment, or conduct research?

○ Does the lesson move at a brisk pace?

○ Do you acknowledge work well done when assignments are completed?

Feeling

○ Do you state a potential benefit to the students or others in your stated purpose of the lesson?

○ Do you include in your presentation ways the new learning can help people?

○ Do you greet students when they enter the class, make them feel welcome and happy to be in your class?

○ Do you establish a relationship with each student in your class?

○ Do you provide ongoing feedback to students as they work?

○ Are there opportunities for students to work cooperatively in completing an activity or assignment?

○ Do you acknowledge the personal contributions of the students to the success of the lesson?

Judging

- ◯ Have you included in your lesson a statement about the purpose of the lesson and an overview of the plan for the day?
- ◯ Have you included specific information about expectations for assignments and due dates?
- ◯ Have you included a summary at the end of your lesson, including a reminder of assignments due and a brief outline of the plan for the following day?
- ◯ Have you prepared long-range plans for your class and outlined these plans for your students?

Perceiving

- ◯ Have you included options for assignments that allow students to make a choice of the task they complete?
- ◯ Have you provided opportunities for flexibility in the manner in which assignments will be completed?
- ◯ Have you allowed for students to exercise a sense of curiosity during the lesson?
- ◯ Do you sometimes change the plan for the day because of special situations or to take advantage of other opportunities for students?

RESOURCES

RESOURCE 6, *Engaging Students of All Types*, puts these questions into a handy crib-sheet form.

So far, we have been discussing areas of instruction, an area where teachers typically have the most control. However, there is an area where teachers are often more at the mercy of patterns that students have developed elsewhere: how students use their time and go about their assignments.

Time Management and Work Habits

Time management and work habits are behaviors developed from a number of overlapping factors of innate predispositions and environmental encounters. Research, as well as experience, indicates the significant impact type preferences have internally and behaviorally on a person's orientation to time.[3]

Every teacher has reported at one time or another to parents, "Your son can do the work; he just doesn't apply himself." Or, "Your daughter knows the material; she just doesn't stay on task." Otto Kroeger has suggested that all types procrastinate most when they are called on to use the opposites of their type preferences.[4] How students (and teachers) manage their time during the school day is a critical factor in how much learning takes place, and our own research indicates that this varies considerably by type.

Beginning with Extraversion and Introversion, teachers can use their awareness of differences to allow students to spend at least half of their time in their preferred attitude. Extraverts gain mental energy by using time in the outer world of action and interaction. Introverts gain mental energy by using time in the inner world of reflection and time away from others. In the classroom, this means teachers are wise to allow students to have time and space for interactive learning and discussion and fairly equal time and space for individual reflection and work. However, when a choice must be made, it may be prudent to err on the side of Extraversion. One researcher working with young adolescents suggests that because students of this age are adapting to peers, their Introversion may be masked by an Extraverted attitude.[5]

The following questions and statements show how the different preferences relate to managing time:

Extraversion (E) Time is for action and interaction.

Introversion (I) Time is for thinking about something.

Sensing (S) What can I experience or know concretely about this present moment?

Intuition (N) What are new possibilities to be discovered and explored in this and the succeeding moments?

Thinking (T) How can I use this moment independently to make logical sense of something?

Feeling (F) How can I use this moment for values as I've acquired them from past experiences?

Judging (J) Time is a finite resource to be organized and controlled like other resources.

Perceiving (P) Time is to be experienced to the fullest and implies adaptation to the present moment.

"Preparation, I have often said, is rightly two-thirds of any venture."

AMELIA EARHART (1897–1937) This American pilot was the first woman to perform a solo flight across the Atlantic. She disappeared over the Pacific while attempting a solo flight around the world.

Reported Comments About Time Management

Interestingly, the following information we've gathered from students and teachers was reported by the types *regardless* of their preference for Extraversion or Introversion. It seems that how one uses time to perceive and make judgments is consistent with all the other information we have presented thus far regarding ST, SF, NF, and NT whether this occurs in the extraverted or introverted world. However, adding the fourth dichotomy of Judging ("Joy in Closure") and Perceiving ("Joy in Process")[6] adds a distinctive change in the behaviors practiced in learning.

Sensing, Thinking, and Judging (STJ)

- Like to plan, organize, schedule, and use objective data.
- Will work toward a given deadline spacing work out from date of assignment to due date.
- Do not like interruptions or changes to interfere with planned use of time.
- Likely to complete a task or responsibility before relaxing or playing and expect others to do the same. Little tolerance when extracurricular activities interrupt or interfere with academics.
- Students want clear, goal-oriented instructions that spell out precisely and concisely what the teacher expects and when the teacher expects it in order to organize time in step-by-step increments.
- Teachers will give precise instructions with less room for individual input.
- Teachers will likely plan for contingencies and expect students to do the same.
- Teachers have little tolerance when extracurricular activities interrupt or interfere with academics.
- Teachers tend to expect all students to follow the same procedures and regulations. May have little tolerance for individual exceptions.

Sensing, Thinking, and Perceiving (STP)

- Want to experience present-time reality.
- Like to use time for producing immediate, visible results.
- Likely to use time efficiently if there's an immediate, practical, or concrete problem to be solved, and they are allowed to solve it in their own way.
- Most energized at the last minute against a deadline.
- Students likely to wait until the last minute before undertaking a long-term assignment.
- Teachers not likely to give long-term assignments unless required by the curriculum.

Sensing, Feeling, and Judging (SFJ)

- Want to use time to meet others' needs in a practical way.
- Like to structure time. Will spend time getting resources organized before beginning a task.
- May procrastinate on assignments that do not have a personal connection.
- Conscientious about deadlines.
- Will work toward a given deadline, spacing their work out from date of assignment to due date.
- Students want clear, goal-oriented instructions that spell out precisely and concisely what the teacher wants and when the teacher wants it in order to organize time in step-by-step increments.
- Teachers likely to give precise instructions which allow for some individual input within prescribed parameters.

Sensing, Feeling, and Perceiving (SFP)

- Want to experience time for personal benefit or enjoyment.
- Have relaxed attitude about time.
- Likely to retain learning that has been experienced directly. Take time to memorize facts in assignments that need to be retained, but have not been experienced directly.
- Likely to procrastinate on long-term assignments—even more so if they deal with theories or analysis.
- Students likely to use time more efficiently when involved with much sensory data.
- Students likely to use time less efficiently when involved primarily with words (reading or writing) since words are symbols that require translation into meaning.

Intuition, Feeling, and Judging (NFJ)

- Want to use time for ideas that affect people.

- Keenly aware of future time.

- Like time structured, but resist having it structured by someone else.

- Students likely to feel a pull between wanting to use time to pursue options and wanting to bring about closure to a task. Thus, they may begin work on an assignment immediately then wait until the last minute to pull it together.

- Teachers likely to give long-term assignments with deadlines but not require that work be turned in incrementally.

- Teachers may be tolerant of students asking for personal exceptions to deadlines, and students may assume that they will be willing to make exceptions.

Intuition, Feeling, and Perceiving (NFP)

- Want to spend time exploring possibilities for people.

- Like to use time to experience as many opportunities as possible, so may be distracted from one experience to another or from what seems more like a task to what seems more like an opportunity.

- Likely to resist deadlines. May view deadlines as barriers to creativity.

- Want to structure own time and may resist anyone else trying to do so.

- Tolerant of missed deadlines and expect others to be so also.

- Use time most efficiently when there is an inspiration or insight to follow so tend to work with bursts of energy.

- May procrastinate on producing a finished product.

- Assignments without an element of personal discovery may seem more like a task.

Intuition, Thinking, and Judging (NTJ)

- View time as linear—the present moment relates to the past and to the future.
- Like to use time to problem-solve situations that fit into a grand scheme—the more complex, the better.
- Want to structure own time and are likely to do so. Resist others prescribing how time should be managed.
- May be distracted by new possibilities and opportunities and take on more than can be accomplished in a given amount of time.
- Students use their time initially to determine ultimate goals, and then use remaining time to explore components involved in achieving goals, pulling it all together at the last minute.
- Teachers tend to give problems to be solved by a certain time with the expectation that students will organize their own time. Thus, there are few, if any, step-by-step instructions.

Intuition, Thinking, and Perceiving (NTP)

- Want to experience time exploring ideas. See time itself as an idea.
- Likely to view deadlines as barriers to creativity.
- Want to order own time and may ignore others' attempts to do this for them.
- Students likely to want to spend their time doing more thinking than acting. May procrastinate on producing a final product.
- Teachers likely to focus on the quality use of time for an assignment rather than be concerned about quantity. Thus, assignments tend to be more global and longer range—even semester long.

RESOURCES

RESOURCE 8, *Type and Time*, provides handouts on the effects of these type preferences regarding time management.

Should Students and Teachers Be Matched by Type?

The question often arises whether, given the research data, students should be matched with teachers of their own type. In general, our recommendation, and that of most other type professionals, is a resounding, "Not usually!" Students live in a world that requires the use of all the functions, not just their own preferences. We all need to be able to communicate with, influence, cooperate with, complement, learn from, and live with people of all types. While we have natural type preferences, we develop all the preferences from activities we engage in and from the people with whom we observe and interact. In school as elsewhere we need each other because of our differences.

Sometimes, however, when a student is struggling and seems disconnected from the teacher, it can be advisable to place that student with a teacher whose type matches the student's. While type differences may not be the cause of the problems, there is the possibility that a teacher of the same type will connect more readily with the way that student's mind is engaged and may also be able to communicate better with the student. If a more positive connection, either academic or personal, is made with this student, the self-affirmation produced by such a relationship could help turn the student around.

To Wrap It Up

Understanding that some students may use the cognitive processes of perception (Sensing and Intuition) and judgment (Thinking and Feeling) in ways different from their own, teachers can strive to personalize instruction and engage students' minds through natural preferences. Personalizing instruction, while presenting a teacher with new challenges, offers the rewards of increased motivation, higher achievement, greater self-concept, and fewer discipline problems. It's not a bad investment!

In a Nutshell

- Minds respond differently—students do not all learn the same way and teachers do not all teach in the same way. Teachers and students can learn to recognize their own natural mental processes and learn to talk about type preferences.

- ST focuses on accomplishing factual or tangible tasks efficiently.

- SF focuses on meeting the practical needs of people or on personal creative endeavors.

- NF focuses on human growth and development and self-expression.

- NT focuses on analytical problem solving.

- Teachers can most successfully engage students' minds through the students' natural preferences.

- Personalizing words of instruction and learning activities based on personality type engages students for maximum achievement.

- Type preferences impact a student's use of time.

- All types are more likely to procrastinate when they are asked to use the opposites of their type preferences.

- Teachers can use choice based on type as a powerful motivator to increase student engagement.

Check Your Understanding

Q *Which type of mind (ST, SF, NF, NT) is most likely to be motivated by the following words?*
  1) Pretend, Create
  2) Fix, Make
  3) Share, Visit
  4) Analyze, Solve
A 1) NF; 2) ST; 3) SF; 4) NT

Q *Which type of mind (ST, SF, NF, NT) is likely to be most motivated by the following activities?*
  1) independent learning, debates, research projects
  2) show and tell, small-group projects, writing about a real personal experience
  3) noncompetitive games, role-plays, creative projects
  4) physical competitions, building things, laboratory experiments
A 1) NT; 2) SF; 3) NF; 4) ST

- Choose a good lesson you have already developed. Review it to see if you have allowed for Extraversion and Introversion differences by including interactive learning and discussion as well as time for individual reflection and work. Chances are you have. However, if not, see if there are ways you can tweak the lesson to allow for both external and internal stimuli.

- If you are feeling really motivated, compare this same lesson with the kinds of learning activities that appeal most to the different types as noted in table 2.c, Engaging Learning Activities and in Resource 2, *Learning Preferences by Type: Words and Activities that Work*. Evaluate how well you cover all four sets of preference groupings. Are there additional ways you can teach the lesson to engage students who may be less engaged? (Resource 6, *Engaging Students of All Types*, is a helpful resource for planning lessons.)

- If you have students who are not engaged productively in your classroom, select one of them, and based on the information in this chapter do one of the following:

    ‣ If it is possible, discuss with the student some of the learning differences discussed in chapter 1 and summarized in Resource 1, *Type Preferences and Learning: A Quick Reference Guide*, and experiment with a learning activity that seems to correspond best with his or her mind. See table 2.e in this chapter for some suggestions.

    ‣ If a direct discussion isn't fruitful, use clues from Resource 1 to form a working hypothesis on what that student's preferences may be. Experiment with learning activities that correspond with your hypothesis using your own ideas or suggestions found in table 2.e.

CHAPTER 2

Personalizing

Instruction

GREAT MINDS

"The task of the educator lies in seeing that the child does not confound good with immobility and evil with activity."

MARIA MONTESSORI (1870–1952) The Italian physician developed a method for educating children that involved treating them as individuals and giving them appropriate learning materials and a classroom environment to aid them on their journey of discovery. Her methods continue to be widely practiced in educational settings.

Personalizing the Learning Environment

Personalization: . . . [is] providing students with opportunities to develop a sense of belonging to the school, a sense of ownership over the direction of one's learning, the ability to recognize options, and to make choices based on one's experience and understanding of the options.

Breaking Ranks II: Strategies for Leading High School Reform[1]

According to David Sousa, author of *How the Brain Learns,* self-concept is defined as "our perception of who we are and how we fit into the world."[2] According to Dr. Sousa, self-concept determines in large measure whether a student will accept or reject new learning as the brain processes whether an experience is positive or negative. Therefore, to create an environment that will stimulate rather than shut-down learning for students, effective teachers need to work with the different kinds of mental processing represented by the types. Teachers who ignore these differences are likely to find their students struggling, confused, or unmotivated, the result of which is often "acting out" behavior or withdrawal. Many incidents of student distraction or misbehavior can be prevented if the learning environment is personalized to meet the differing environmental needs of the students in the classroom.

Optimal Learning Environment

To learn how the types learn best, we went directly to the different types to learn from the "experts." Students in numerous workshops have provided us with the following information about what they need for an optimal learning environment.

Sensing and Thinking (ST)

- An orderly, structured environment.
- Problem solving, fact-based instruction.
- Learning of specific skills.
- Clear goals and step-by-step instruction for tasks.
- A controlled, familiar environment.
- Concrete resources with which to work.
- No frequent change.

Sensing and Feeling (SF)

- A warm and friendly environment.
- The teacher takes a personal interest in students.
- Clear goals and precise instructions.
- An organized environment.
- An environment that fosters interactive work in small groups.

Intuition and Feeling (NF)

- A warm and supportive environment.
- A feeling of connection with the teacher.
- Interaction with other students.
- Goals that allow for individual input into the process.
- Flexibility in procedures to be followed.
- Frequent feedback.

Intuition and Thinking (NT)

- A mentally stimulating environment.
- Goals that pose challenging questions or problems to be solved.
- Freedom to work toward goals independently or with one or two others.
- Resources for independent work.
- No routine.
- Limited rules and regulations.
- A variety of activities.

RESOURCES

RESOURCE 9, *Type and Work Space,* provides a reproducible copy of these differences.

Use of Physical Space

In addition, type preferences affect the *space* needs of students differently. At the elementary and middle school levels, many of these individual needs have been accommodated by the structure of the buildings themselves as well as by teachers within the classroom. This is less true at the high school level where the desks in many classrooms are arranged in rows with the focus on the teacher giving a lecture at the front of the room.

Reports from the types indicate that desired use of space is particularly affected by the basic orientations of Extraversion and Introversion and the four processes of Sensing (S), Intuition (N), Thinking (T), and Feeling (F).

Extraversion: *Space that allows for interaction—sometimes with one other person; sometimes with a group—without having to be concerned about disturbing others.*

Introversion: *Private space for reflection and individual work, free from sensory distractions.*

Sensing and Thinking (ST)

• Neat and orderly space with all materials in place.

• Some compact space that is personal.

• Space that lends itself to action.

• Easily accessible equipment or information sources.

• Clear desk or table tops on which to work.

• Space geared more for function than form.

Sensing and Feeling (SF)

• Space for personal contact with others.

• Sensory input needs to be present and personally pleasing—e.g., varied colors, textures, sounds.

• Overall atmosphere of neatness without uniform orderliness.

• Space where personal work can be displayed or that exhibits the contribution to the learning community.

• Décor that suggests a sense of community or family.

Intuition and Feeling (NF)

- Personal space where it's OK to clutter.

- Space for meeting and working with others.

- Space for personal expression—e.g., display of work accomplished or work in progress; artifacts or decorations that represent themselves or the classroom community as they like to envision it.

- Private space free of interruptions and sensory input when individual concentration is essential for task accomplishment.

- Space where form is as important as function.

- Space to save anything that either has personal meaning or has a possible future use.

Intuition and Thinking (NT)

- Space for independent work.

- Opportunity to work individually at a computer.

- "Expansive" space if needed to explore new ideas.

- Opportunity to see the classroom as the whole school or community— or beyond!

- Easy access to books and other reference materials.

- Space to organize materials into stacks by categories.

There are two compelling reasons why all four of these type-combinations should be accommodated in the use of classroom space:

- All four type-combinations likely are present in each classroom.

- All types access their opposite preferences from time to time suggesting that their environmental needs may vary.

RESOURCES

RESOURCE 9, *Type and Work Space,* provides a summary of these different space needs.

Negotiating "Learning Community" Space

Designing the classroom environment to accommodate type differences addresses some of the key factors in personalizing the learning environment. As a result of taking into consideration all types of learners, the environment will be student-centered. Students will feel supported and know that the teacher cares about them and wants them to succeed; they will feel a sense of belonging and feel connected to their teacher; they will know their individual interests and needs are being addressed; and they will feel they have choices and control over their learning.

Therefore, negotiations about school environments can become an important component of both the learning process and of the building of a learning community. Here are two suggested ways a teacher can approach this task:

- Discuss with students the various activities that are likely to take place in the classroom during the school year and ask them to design how they would like their classroom to be arranged to accommodate these activities. A committee of students, working with the teacher, can discuss the ideas suggested and propose one or more designs that incorporate the various ideas. In the case of a high school situation where different teachers might use a room at different class times, the teachers who use the room can compile the suggestions presented by each group of students and arrive at a decision that is acceptable to all groups. If consensus is not possible, the decision could be to change the arrangement of the room at the end of each grading period or semester.

- The teacher can turn the issue of the design of classroom space into a learning activity. Such an undertaking offers the teacher the opportunity to teach problem-solving skills at the same time the class is building a sense of community. As students discuss various aspects of the use of space, they share their personal learning environment needs with others in the class. This discussion provides a mechanism for students to realize that they do not all share the same preferences for use of physical space, and it lets them know that they will not be forced to work in only one kind of environment.

Managing Student Behavior

A positive learning environment is one in which students are focused and engaged. In such environments, incidents of inappropriate student behavior are few and far between; and when they occur they are handled promptly and appropriately. Maintaining this kind of climate in the classroom can be a challenge, and a teacher may need a variety of tools to accomplish the task.

Table 3.a *Report from Students About Discipline*

	What are some reasons students of your type might get in trouble in school?	*What advice do you have regarding strategies teachers can use to help you get back on task?*
Sensing & Thinking (ST)	Lack of attention Frustration with trying to be perfect Not being cooperative Not doing homework Giving in to pressure from peers Frustration of overachieving	Talk to me on my level Encourage me Show interest Don't single me out Don't compare me to others Don't treat me like a child
Sensing & Feeling (SF)	Talking in class Letting others take advantage of me Going along with friends	Ask about me personally Do not yell at me Do not embarrass me Do not use sarcasm
Intuition & Feeling (NF)	Not paying attention in class—mind wandering Speaking out in class to get a point across Not giving other students a turn (Extraverts) Not thinking before talking (Extraverts) Problems with authority Not following the rules	Ask questions Get me involved Speak to me privately Don't lecture or yell at me Don't embarrass me Don't single me out Don't be disrespectful
Intuition & Thinking (NT)	Being bored with the class Daydreaming instead of paying attention Talking instead of listening Not being challenged Challenging the teacher	Talk to me privately Engage my mind in what's happening in the class Give me some time to "cool off" Be straight and to the point Let me know I will not be taken advantage of Don't use "put downs" or degrade me Don't yell or create a scene

Type differences account for only some of the reasons that students misbehave or are distracted. However, the effectiveness of discipline strategies will vary depending on students' types; therefore, type provides a significant mechanism for analyzing and diagnosing student behavior, as well as a tool for inducing change. Leverne Barrett, a researcher who studied classroom environment, found that "by understanding personality type theory, teachers at all levels can begin to understand cause and effect in the classroom and begin to diagnose and analyze behaviors that reduce learning."[3]

For our research, we went to classrooms and talked with students of various types about possible causes of discipline problems and ways teachers could effectively handle the situation so students could get back on track (table 3.a).

Significantly, even though these students had very limited type knowledge, their responses are consistent with type differences as described here:

- The ST types, who typically are motivated by a technical task and driven by efficiency, will find little use for anything that slows them down or seems inefficient—whether that barrier be too much talk, people, or homework.

- The SF types, who are especially attuned to making their environments harmonious, are caught between cooperating with their teachers and the pull of a relationship with their friends.

- The NF types, whose minds see possibilities in just about everything on earth and want all creatures on that earth to be equal in rank, are not likely to remain silent when a treasured value is in question nor stay tuned when tangential associations are exploding in their minds.

- The NT types, who "do not suffer fools gladly," will sooner or later challenge the authority of a teacher in the absence of what they consider a sufficiently challenging mental exercise.

Preventing Discipline Problems

First, let's review the ways students of different types learn most easily and the type of learning environment in which this occurs. Then we will explore what frustrates students that may lead to discipline problems. There is an obvious connection between learning environment and behavior—giving teachers another area over which they have some control.

ST Students

ST students learn most easily when

- There is structure and order.
- Learning is practical and relevant.
- The teacher explains things step-by-step in sequential order.
- Learning is hands-on.
- The five senses are engaged.
- Facts are used for a logical purpose.
- Concrete instruction precedes abstract concepts.
- Recognition comes after a task is accomplished rather than all through the process.

In the preferred learning environment

- Procedures, rules, and routines are in place, known by students, and consistently enforced by the teacher.
- The teacher promptly addresses any behavior that is not in keeping with the procedures and expectations.
- There is order and structure in the classroom.
- There are clear expectations for behavior and assignments.
- There are no vague directions or teachers "winging it."

May become frustrated and a discipline problem when

- There are distractions and interruptions to normal procedures.
- There seems to be little or no relevance to practical problem solving.

Strategic Intervention

- Give them a specific, concrete task that keeps them actively engaged towards a goal.
- Establish classroom procedures.

Application Scenario. Thomas had never really liked math, and geometry class was no exception. He just didn't care about learning how to prove theorems and he didn't see how being able to prove triangles were congruent would help him get a job. He wanted to learn things that were practical and useful in the real world. Furthermore, his teacher always seemed to be changing things around. One day she'd start class with a new lesson and then another day she'd go over homework first. She'd announce a test for a particular day and he'd study for it and then she'd say she had changed her mind and they'd have the test "sometime next week."

When the teacher assigned a class project to design and construct something useful such as a bird house using at least three geometric shapes, Thomas proved to be one of the most interested and hardest workers. The hands-on learning project actually provided him with the structure that the teacher had not been able to provide.

Note: While students with a preference for STP do like to have the basic ST structures in place, their tolerance for structure and routine is limited. They often thrive when they are attracted by an unexpected concrete problem needing immediate attention. So much so, that they may create such a problem if there is not enough frequent hands-on activity in the learning process. When this occurs, their natural gift of realistic resourcefulness in the face of trouble comes into play and they go into immediate action. And as a result, they may leave behind rules and routines. It is the wise teacher who can understand that some of this unexpected activity is "troubleshooting." Many of these students later find very satisfying careers as emergency medical workers, fire fighters, or mechanical engineers. Meanwhile, back in the classroom, teachers need to offer these students a learning environment of hands-on problem solving as frequently as is reasonably possible.

SF Students

SF students learn most easily when

- There are goals and precise instructions.
- There is structure.
- Learning is practical and relevant for the here-and-now lives of people.
- The teacher relates to students individually.
- There is frequent feedback.
- It is possible to work with specifics that deal with people.
- Working with a friend.
- There are activities involving the five senses.
- Models or demonstrations are provided.
- Concrete specifics precede an abstract concept or "the big picture."

In the preferred learning environment

- Things are organized and neat.
- There is a warm, supportive, and harmonious climate.
- There is interactive one-on-one work with a friend or work in small harmonious groups is possible.
- A visually attractive environment engages the senses.

May become frustrated and a discipline problem when

- They feel ignored by the teacher.
- They are required to work under too much time pressure.

Strategic Intervention

- Show personal interest in the student.
- Give the student a task to work on with a friend or a task that will help the teacher or class in some way.

Application Scenario. Susan sat near two of her best friends in her middle school English class. She frequently found herself writing notes to them when she should have been paying attention to the teacher. Because the three friends sat close to each other, they also frequently talked in class, especially when the teacher's back was turned or when the teacher asked students to work independently on a class assignment. Susan thought the teacher didn't like her. On several occasions Susan had raised her hand to ask a question or for some help and the teacher ignored her. The teacher noticed Susan talking to her friends and not paying attention.

The teacher arranged a private conversation with Susan and learned of a difficult situation at home. She listened with understanding, assuring Susan she understood how it was hard to stay focused and said she would like to help any way she could. She negotiated with Susan to allow for a group assignment with her friends. Susan agreed to make a greater effort to pay attention in class.

GREAT MINDS

"True strength can never be derived only from talent but from the courageous struggle with difficulties. Whoever overcomes wins."

ALFRED ADLER (1870–1937) This Austrian-born medical doctor was a colleague of Sigmund Freud who broke from Freud's circle to develop a separate field of therapeutic psychology. Alder's approach incorporates social relationships into the explanation for psychological difficulties, including Alder's original concept of inferiority complex.

NF Students

NF students learn most easily when

- Learning is personally oriented.
- There are opportunities for communication and working cooperatively.
- There are possibilities and meaning, particularly for people.
- There are opportunities to be creative.
- Goals allow for personal input into the final outcome.
- Learning involves words.
- Abstract concepts or "the big picture" precedes concrete specifics.

In the preferred learning environment

- There is a harmonious environment where all students feel accepted and included.
- The students are not ridiculed and the teacher does not use sarcasm.
- There are no conflicts or arguments.
- The classroom is run on a democratic model.
- There is a caring and warm atmosphere between students and between the students and the teacher.
- Personal relationships are valued.
- The teacher provides frequent personal recognition and feedback.

May become frustrated and a discipline problem when

- Students' feelings are not considered and students are belittled or humiliated in front of the class.
- Rules are too rigid and do not take individual circumstances into account.
- Work does not allow for individual creativity.

Strategic Intervention

- Get the student involved in an activity or task that will benefit others or encourage some personal creativity.

Applications Scenario. Sam disliked his Spanish class. He knew he needed the course for college but some things really concerned him. The teacher had very strict rules and never deviated from them even when there were special circumstances. The assignments always followed the same format. Study the vocabulary, do the translation, and answer the questions, study for the quiz. They seldom had a chance to be creative and do something fun and different with the language. The teacher sometimes ridiculed students in front of the class when they didn't have their homework done or couldn't answer a question.

Finally, when Sam was frustrated enough, he decided to let the teacher know that Julia, one of the students she was criticizing publicly for incomplete homework, had a mother in the hospital, which meant that Julia had to cook meals and take care of the younger children in the family. Further, he told the teacher he wished the classes had more creative activities. The teacher thanked him for letting her know and suggested Sam could become a Spanish tutor for Julia, perhaps devising a creative way to help her keep up in class. Sam also came up with the idea of letting all the students create stories using new vocabulary words, the stories actually to be read to elementary classes. The teacher agreed to try it.

NT Students

NT students learn most easily when

- There is order but limited rules and routines.
- They are mentally challenged.
- Creativity and thinking are encouraged.
- Teachers ask "why" and present problems for students to solve or discuss.
- High standards are in place and mediocre work is not acceptable.
- Abstract concepts or "the big picture" precede concrete specifics.
- They are recognized after a task is accomplished rather than throughout the process.

In the preferred learning environment

- A stimulating environment helps students feel challenged and inspired.
- Students are able to pursue their own creative instincts.
- The teacher recognizes and acknowledges competence and independent thinking.
- The teacher is receptive to students' suggestions for improvements.
- Abstract concepts precede the concrete specifics.

May become frustrated and a discipline problem when

- There is too much drill and repetition.
- They feel the teacher is wasting valuable time.
- There are too many routines.
- Rules do not make sense and inhibit independent learning.
- They feel the teacher is "talking down" to them as if they were incompetent.

Strategic Intervention

- Give students an intellectual challenge that acknowledges their competence.

Applications Scenario. Sharon did not enjoy her biology class. The teacher spent at least ten minutes at the beginning of each class taking roll and "shooting the breeze" with the students. He went over the answer to every homework question, even the easy questions. Sharon was often bored and found herself not paying attention. She let her mind wander in class or made comments to students who sat near her, and her grades were falling.

Sharon's attitude made a 180-degree turn when the teacher announced that the class could work with a partner on an independent project and they could choose the project from a list he had prepared. Sharon quickly asked Mark, who seemed to like a challenge, if he would be her partner. They worked together and produced a video on the complexities of genetic counseling for a couple with a family history of cystic fibrosis.

RESOURCES

RESOURCE 10, *Preventing Discipline Problems*, provides information to help teachers develop strategies for preventing discipline problems. RESOURCE 11, *How Would You Intervene?* (three case studies), is an exercise which can be used to help teachers build skills in exploring interventions based on type.

Minimizing Discipline Issues. Additional resources to help teachers minimize discipline problems can be found in the resource section of this handbook. These resources can assist the teacher to keep students motivated and engaged in the learning process.

- For a general summary of learning differences by type, see Resource 1, *Type Preferences and Learning: A Quick Reference Guide.*
- To motivate students with type in the delivery of instruction, see Resource 2, *Learning by Type: Words and Activities that Work,* and Resource 6, *Engaging Students of All Types.*
- To encourage student self-assessment, see Resource 14, *Student Self-Assessment,* which includes subject specific as well as general guides for self-assessment.
- To ask students to self-report their learning needs and when they might get into difficulty, see Resource 17, *To do My Best Work I Need...*
- To involve students in the design and arrangement of learning space, see Resource 9, *Type and Work Space.*

- To help students respect different types of people, see **Resource 1**, *Type Preferences and Learning: A Quick Reference Guide*.
- Consider explaining the rudiments of type to students in the context of understanding how students learn in different but equally good ways and, therefore, have different needs in the classroom. Perhaps involve a school counselor or other teachers who know type.

To Wrap It Up

Personalizing the learning environment, while presenting a teacher with new challenges, offers the rewards of increased motivation, higher achievement, greater self-concepts, and fewer discipline problems. It's not a bad investment!

In a Nutshell

- To create an environment that stimulates rather than shuts down learning for students, effective teachers need to work with the different kinds of mental processing represented by the types.
- Preferred learning environments vary by type.
  - Extraverts prefer time and space for interacting with others.
  - Introverts prefer private time and space for reflection and individual work.
  - Sensing Thinking types prefer clear expectations for behavior and assignments; hands-on learning.
  - Sensing Feeling types prefer neat, warm, supportive, and harmonious environments; a visually appealing environment that engages the senses; opportunities to work with a friend or in a small group.
  - Intuitive Feeling types prefer harmonious, caring environments where all students feel accepted and included; they want the teacher to recognize and appreciate them in a personal way with frequent feedback.
  - Intuitive Thinking types prefer stimulating environments where students feel intellectually challenged and inspired and are able to pursue their own creative instincts; the teacher is receptive to students' suggestions for improvements.
  - Judging types prefer organized environments related to time, space, and lessons.
  - Perceiving types prefer flexible and adaptable environments that allow for spontaneity.

- Type provides a significant mechanism for analyzing and diagnosing student behavior as well as a useful tool for inducing change in student behavior.

Applications Scenario. Ricky did not enjoy his history class and often found it hard to concentrate. Sometimes Ricky got into trouble because he found it hard to sit still and take notes about events that happened a long time ago. Ricky didn't see any reason to memorize all those dates.

Q *If Ricky's teacher wanted to improve the situation and hypothesized that Ricky's type might be ENFP what is an intervention she might try to engage Ricky's mind more effectively?*

A The teacher could get Ricky involved in an activity or task that would encourage some personal creativity. An example might be an independent project in which he would explore the impact of historical events either on the arts or people's daily lives during the time period being studied. The project could be presented to the class in a manner of Ricky's choosing such as a debate, role-play, PowerPoint presentation, or other visual or auditory presentation. The teacher could give him the opportunity to work alone or with other students.

Applications Scenario. A teacher who knows type has a student coming late to class for three consecutive days.

Q *Which of the following approaches is the teacher likely to use if she wants to change the behavior and believes her student is (a) a Thinking type or (b) a Feeling type?*

Response 1: "I need your help with a concern. You've come late to class for the last three days. Is there something going on I should know about?"

Response 2: "You've now been late to class for the last three days. You know we expect students to be in class on time so they don't miss any valuable instruction. Can you tell me why you've been late?"

A **Response 1 Feeling type:** The focus is on the student and the student's individual circumstances. Both the personal concern shown by the teacher as well as the desire for harmony with the teacher is likely to result in more cooperation from the student.

Response 2 Thinking type: The focus is on the principle involved, something to which the Thinking function is more likely to respond. The personal appeal of the first response might be received as patronizing by a Thinking type. In the event there is a valid personal reason that warrants concern, a Thinking type is not likely to be personally offended by the focus on the principle, whereas that same mention of the school's expectation may evoke defensiveness in a Feeling type.

Getting Started

Review a lesson that was less successful with some students and compare the lesson's design and delivery, and the classroom environment, with some of the reasons students become disengaged in class:

- **STs:** May feel the lesson lacks relevance and isn't practical; does not include hands-on learning.
- **SFs:** May feel ignored by the teacher. Friends exert influence and get student off task.
- **NFs:** Rules do not take individual circumstances into account; student's feelings are not considered; work does not allow for individual creativity.
- **NTs:** Too much drill and repetition and lack of intellectual challenge; rules do not make logical sense.

Rework the lesson to accommodate the types with lesson content and delivery and classroom environment issues. See Resources 1, 4, 6, and 9 for clues and suggestions.

4

Personalizing Assessment

Students differ not only in how they prefer to take in and process information but also in how they best demonstrate their learning.

JAY MCTIGHE and KEN O'CONNOR
Educational Leadership

Assessment has traditionally been (and continues to be) equated with accountability. As a result, formal testing has been the norm for assessment and indeed has become the benchmark to evaluate not only students but also teachers, schools, districts, states, and even entire countries! ("No pressure—just be aware that how you do on this test helps determine your teacher's pay! And the reputation of the school, too!") Yet it's the rare teacher who relies exclusively on formal testing for evaluating a student. Most teachers combine both formal and informal approaches. Acknowledging type differences indeed *necessitates* that a variety of assessment approaches be used if students are to have fair and equal opportunities to demonstrate learning. In table 4.a (page 63), note the differences among what students (organized by preferences) reported to us as the means by which they believe they can best demonstrate their knowledge.

Developing Criteria for Evaluation

Regardless of the method used for formal evaluation of students (paper and pencil tests, portfolio evaluation, etc.), the best assessment is based on a set of criteria for determining level of performance that is clearly defined, is fair and based on a standard of excellence, is uniform for all students, and can be interpreted to students and others with clarity. Use of Sensing, Intuition, Thinking, and Feeling provides a framework for developing these criteria.

Step 1 Sensing

- Review stated objectives for the learning.

- Obtain and review existing samples completed by experts in the field that represent fulfillment of the objectives.

- Review samples of students' work ranging from poor to excellent.

- Find the standards required for the next higher level in this course (e.g., next level high school or college).

Step 2 Intuition

- Brainstorm what criteria or standards you believe are important in a quality product.

- Brainstorm what might be innovative points or features a student could add that would go beyond the explicit requirements of the stated objectives. (Such additions could be given extra credit.)

- Consider standards for the process as well as the product. (Caution: Leave room for students of different types to approach a task in different, but equally beneficial ways.)

Step 3 Thinking

- Determine which possible outcomes are expected based on the objectives and are feasible for accomplishment.

- Arrange criteria for judging performance on a continuum from low to high based on information obtained (see Sensing).

- Establish a rating scale to reflect these various levels of accomplishment in relation to what you and other experts consider clear excellence. Include a scale for additional or innovative points or features as well as the minimum acceptable level of accomplishment.

Step 4 Feeling

- Determine if criteria for judging performance are meaningful to students, parents, and others who are involved.

- Evaluate criteria for gender, ethnic bias.

- Consider how understandable the interpretation of the rating scale is to students and parents and others.

- Get feedback from colleagues and students on the criteria established.

RESOURCES

RESOURCE 12, *Developing Assessment Criteria: A Guide for Teachers*, contains a summary of these points.

Table 4.a *Students Report on Assessment Preferences*

Sensing and Thinking (ST)	Sensing and Feeling (SF)	Intuition and Feeling (NF)	Intuition and Thinking (NT)
Objective tests	Objective tests	Essays	Essays
Criterion-referenced tests	Oral reports	Observation of how engaged in learning	Opportunity to demonstrate critical thinking skills
Mastery tests	Teacher observation of use of what has been learned	Critique of individual or team project	Critique of an independent project
Demonstrate knowledge with application	No time limit on testing	Open-ended questions	Open-ended questions
No time limit on testing			

Accommodating Type Differences in Assessment

Rather than argue the merits of the plethora of high stakes tests that today's students face, we will acknowledge their reality, assume they have a role to play, and discuss the impact of type on testing questions and answers. We will also indulge our own biases by mentioning that more emphasis be placed on student-centered assessment, as we believe that student-centered forms of assessment reflect most closely the accountability that young people will face in the adult working world.

Within this framework, we include applications for use of type in

1) student centered self-assessment,

2) portfolio assessment,

3) teacher-designed tests, and

4) standardized testing.

Student Centered Self-Assessment

The mental habit of being responsible for one's own learning and development is taught when students set their own standards for achievement before they begin a project or activity, evaluate their strategies and results during the activity, and add their own comments and critique at the completion of each activity. Zessoules and Gardner emphasize the vital skills learned through this process.

"The capacity to step back [and consider one's work is a] kind of mindfulness [that] grows out of the capacity to judge and refine one's work and efforts, before, during, and after one has attempted to accomplish them." [It is this mindfulness that equips the student to confront the] "real world challenges of understanding their work in relation to that of others, to build on their strengths, and to see new possibilities and challenges in their work."[1]

In the world beyond the school, people judge the competence of others through what they've accomplished—a tangible product or a presentation of considered ideas. Knowing this, we all are motivated to some extent to learn, develop, and produce something that allows others to give us feedback on our competence. Through this process, we also learn to develop internal standards that provide a set of criteria for ongoing self-evaluation. What becomes "acceptable" is based on a combination of our own critique and that of others. Why should schools do it differently if we're preparing students for life beyond the school?

Sold on this approach ourselves, we offer two methods for helping students learn to self-assess: 1) the use of ongoing questions and 2) assessment of work in a portfolio. Naturally, we discuss these in the context of how type can enhance this process.

Ongoing Questioning

Assessment is best when it occurs throughout the entire learning process. Teachers who use strategic ongoing questioning while students carry out an assignment model an ongoing evaluation process. Gradually students will internalize this practice of ongoing questioning and adopt its use for themselves. Type theory postulates that wise problem solving involves use of all four of the mental functions of Sensing, Intuition, Thinking, and Feeling, so it makes sense to ask questions that engage all four functions in each activity.

RESOURCES

Both teacher and student versions of these questions are available in RESOURCE 14, *Student Self-Assessment*, which also provides examples of similar questions adapted for science, mathematics, and music performance.

As an example, questions teachers might ask of students to facilitate self-assessment on a writing assignment could include such questions as described in table 4.b.

Table 4.b *Teacher Guide to Help Students Self-Assess Writing*

	Sensing (S)	Intuition (N)	Thinking (T)	Feeling (F)
Before	Does your subject relate to anything you have done before or previously observed? What information do you need to gather? What grammar do you need to remember? When do you want to edit for grammar?	What ideas pop into your mind? What are your first hunches about this topic? With what do you associate this topic? What generalizations can you make about your topic?	Is there a problem you would like to solve? How can you state the problem clearly? What are some possible solutions	What is most important to you about this subject? What do you most want to get across? Would you like to personalize this subject? If so, how?
During	What facts are you using to support your thesis? What is your syntax and/or sequence of events like? Which of the specific words you've used particularly serve your purpose? Are there other words you might try for effect?	What themes do you want to express? Is there a metaphor for what you want to express? How do you characterize your style?	What is your thesis? Have you supported your thesis with clear arguments? What can you state more concisely or with more clarity?	Where would you like to use the personal voice? Is there a way you can put your own uniqueness into the piece?
After	What additional editing could you do to improve your grammar?	What would be another way of saying or presenting your themes?	Have you defended your conclusions logically? How coherently have you expressed your views?	What does your writing reveal about what's most important to you? Have you supported your values as clearly as you'd like?

CHAPTER 4

Personalizing

Assessment

Hopefully, by now some of the key words associated with each of the four mental functions are becoming imprinted in your mind in such a way that forming your own questions becomes easier. Resource 14 includes a blank master for use with other courses, for specific topics, or for when you would rather use your own questions. As the process of self-assessment becomes more familiar to students, they can be given a copy of this resource and complete it with their own questions before they begin an activity or as their activity progresses through its various stages.

Encourage students to work first with their natural preferences in order to stimulate a natural flow of learning and then direct them to move to questions that engage their less-preferred functions. Engaging the less-preferred functions first often triggers frustration. By listening carefully, the teacher can observe and reinforce not only use of the naturally preferred functions, but also encourage whole mind development as students stretch to the "opposites."

For example, to a student who prefers Intuition to Sensing, the teacher might say, *"I notice you are using more data to back up your assumptions than you did on your last paper. Congratulations!"*

To a student who prefers Thinking to Feeling, the teacher might say, *"I am impressed that you have included your understanding of the consequences of your proposed action on people personally—along with your good logical analysis of societal consequences."*

Added Value if Students Know Type

Teachers who work with students who do not know psychological type as a theory or system nevertheless work with the concepts in their own words without the "labels" of the personality preferences. However, when students already know type, teachers have the benefit of talking with them in a short-hand fashion about the importance of engaging all four mental functions in their learning. For teachers who have this advantage with their students, Resource 14 can be used to help students with self-evaluation. Some suggested ways for using this resource are outlined here:

1. From time to time, give students a copy of the "Sample General Questions" in Resource 14 and ask them to identify at least two questions from each preference category that they will ask themselves as they plan and carry out their assignment.

2. Following completion of an assignment, give students a copy of the Sample General Questions in Resource 14 and ask them to look it over and identify those questions they think they naturally asked themselves while planning and working on their assignment. Ask them to note which categories were left out and may represent blind spots. Suggest that they identify at least two questions from these categories that they will ask themselves on their next project.

3. Once learning activities are selected and plans are made for accomplishing them, either give students the criteria you have developed by which their work will be evaluated or coach *them* through the development of these criteria. Resource 12 can assist with this activity. Ask students to develop questions they will ask themselves for each of the functions before, during, and after the assignment is completed.

4. Draw a chart of four quadrants on a large sheet of paper and post the chart on the wall. Label each of the quadrants as one of the four mental functions. Ask students early in their work, "What questions are you asking of yourself to make this assignment a success?" Write these questions under the function that each most closely represents. Invite students to add new questions as they occur. Announce that each student is expected to add at least one question for each function to the pool of class questions. This exercise alerts students to strengths and potential blind spots they may encounter in completing the assignment.

5. To develop higher-order thinking, at any point during an assignment the teacher may simply ask, "Which questions would be good to ask now?" Students can be referred to the sample questions in Resource 14 for assistance until such questions become more familiar and natural.

Portfolio Assessment

Portfolio presentation, in which students gather and present samples of their work completed over a specified period of time, has increasingly gained acceptance by educators in recent years. High school art and music teachers have used this form of assessment for years when their students have exhibited in juried art shows or performed musical numbers before evaluating committees or juries. In today's schools, elementary and middle school teachers as well as high school teachers of all subjects are employing portfolio presentation as a way to foster self-assessment and "real world" product assessment.

Although teachers can request that all of a student's work be included in the portfolio, the teacher fosters self-assessment when students have a major role in determining *which* samples of their work are to be included. Some ideas for helping students choose the contents are:

- Students choose one or more examples of their early work and one or more examples of their most recent work and include in the presentation an analysis of the difference (rather like preparing for a performance review in a real-life career!).

- Students choose the top ten examples (or another appropriate number) of their work for the presentation and evaluation.

- Students have the option to eliminate up to three pieces of work they do not want included in their presentation and evaluation.

Portfolios can be presented as part of an end-of-year evaluation to allow students to demonstrate their learning and progress. This approach represents a kind of accountability to the learning community of which the student is a part. Many high schools have a graduation requirement of a student-selected senior project carried out under the guidance of a faculty or community advisor. Elementary and middle schools often showcase student portfolios on a special parents' night.

Use of Type-Related Questions for Portfolio Assessment

Questions categorized by mental functions (see table 4.c) are useful for ensuring that students engage all four functions (and thus support whole mind development) even if students do not have formal type knowledge and the "labels" of type are not attached. These questions are also available in Resource 14.

There are any number of ways students and teachers may use these questions to engage each of the four mental processes when evaluating portfolio samples. For example:

- Students can use them to prepare for a portfolio presentation.

- Students can be asked to justify or critique their portfolio selections for themselves or the teacher, using some of the questions as guidelines.

- Teachers can use the questions to query students on their portfolios and, thus, conduct a performance-based evaluation similar to what business managers often do—where both manager and employee provide input.

- Teachers can use the questions as they evaluate their students' portfolios.

- Students can use answers they generate for setting goals for future work.

Table 4.c *Student Guide for Self-Assessment of Portfolio*

Sensing	Intuition
How many samples are in my portfolio?	Is there a pattern to my interests as evidenced by my work?
Do I have enough?	
What information sources have I used?	How would I describe the main "thrust" of what I've developed?
Is my information accurate and thorough?	How would I characterize my writing (or problem solving, model-building, singing, designing, etc.)
What do I observe when I look at, hear, or touch the samples in my portfolio?	
What would someone else likely observe when he or she sees, hears, or touches my work?	How are my samples similar to each other?
	How are my samples different from each other?
What evidence do I see in my work that suggests possible need for improvement or greater knowledge over time?	Which projects came from my own hunches or insights?
	How can I categorize my work for an organized presentation?
	What insights do I have into my learning curve from this collection of my work?
	What other directions could my work take in the future?

Thinking	Feeling
What did I do well?	How do I feel about the collection of work in my portfolio?
How do I describe my strengths as evidenced in this portfolio? Where are they best demonstrated?	What is my unique "stamp" or signature in my work collectively or in any individual piece?
Where are my weaknesses, and how do I describe them?	What does my portfolio tell about me personally?
What changed over time in my work?	Why is that piece (or pieces) meaningful to me?
What do I notice about my work that shows increased learning with each project?	What values of mine are represented in my work?
Which sample of my work demonstrates my best work? Why?	How does my portfolio reveal personal growth through this course?
What made the difference between my best and my least effective pieces?	Who would I most like to see the work in my portfolio?
Have standards I've set for myself evolved or changed? In what way?	
How would I arrange these samples of my work to go from least to most effective?	
How do I evaluate the depth of content represented in my portfolio?	

- The school can host a Portfolio Presentation Week where other students and teachers, parents, members of the board of education, administrators, central office personnel, and community members serve as the audience and have the opportunity to understand personally what is happening in the schools. They can show interest and support for students who will feel proud and accountable to themselves, peers, and adults as they discuss their work and respond to questions.

Teacher-Designed Tests

The information for this section about type and teacher-designed tests is not intended as a comprehensive guide to test construction. What is presented are some ways teachers can incorporate their knowledge of type in their development of tests, especially since education makes this form of assessment such a critical area for students.

Development of Test Questions

Teachers typically put a good deal of energy as well as expertise into the development of test questions; they want their students to have the best opportunity to demonstrate (a) what they have learned and (b) how well they can apply this knowledge. Students typically want to understand the teacher's questions clearly in order to make the highest grade possible. For both objectives to be reached, therefore, the teacher's and students' minds must connect. Unfortunately, this is not as simple as it may seem.

GREAT MINDS

"Teachers, I believe, are the most responsible and important members of society because their professional efforts affect the fate of the earth."

HELEN CALDICOTT (born 1938) An Australian-born pediatrician who was on the faculty of Harvard Medical School before becoming a fulltime anti-nuclear activist has for decades argued against the construction of nuclear weapons and nuclear power plants. A published author, she asserts that nuclear power is more dangerous than is generally accepted.

For example, read the following two versions of the same question—each written by exemplary teachers of senior honors English classes with essentially the same goal in mind.

Teacher 1	Teacher 2
Using one of the books that you have read this semester, pretend you are a psychiatrist trying to analyze one of the characters. What insights do you have even if the character does not have them? What do you think motivates the character to behave as he/she does? What advice would you give this character?	Choose one book that you have read this semester. Select a situation from the book and choose one of the characters to write about. Explain, as if you were a psychiatrist, what you think motivates the unconscious of the character in this situation. As the psychiatrist, what advice would you give this character about his/her behavior in this situation?

The first teacher, Ivan, has a preference for Intuition. He was aware that his students knew the material and had the capability of answering the questions. Yet some of his students struggled to understand what he was asking while others said they had no trouble understanding the questions.

Believing that type preferences could be making a difference, Ivan consulted with a colleague, Sharon, who had a preference for Sensing. Sharon told him frankly that she didn't know what the questions meant! After some further explanation from Ivan (an advantage the students had not had), Sharon re-wrote the assignment. She explained that when questions are written in narrative form, she has to re-read them several times for understanding. This causes an unnecessary loss of time that doesn't occur when the questions are broken into smaller parts. In addition, she said that referencing a specific situation or circumstance would help the questions make sense. Sharon was also less interested in the question when she read the word "pretend," wanting the task to seem more straight-forward than this word suggested. Her final two suggestions were to use more action-oriented verbs, which for her Sensing preference improved the clarity of what the teacher wanted, and to add "white space" between the steps for easier reading. By working together, Ivan and Sharon ensured that the questions were clear to both of them. The questions were also more likely to be clear to both those students with a preference for Sensing and those with a preference for Intuition.

NOTE: *The typical configuration of S–N has been reversed (to N–S) in the examples on pages 71, 73, and 74 to match the text discussion. The typical configuration returns to S–N beginning on page 75.*

"Every great dream begins with a dreamer. Always remember, you have within you the strength, the patience, and the passion to reach for the stars to change the world."

HARRIET TUBMAN (born Armanita Greene, 1820–1913) Born into slavery, on a Maryland plantation, this extraordinary woman, despite harsh injuries as a young person, worked as a nurse during the Civil War, was honored by the Union Army, led as many as 300 people to freedom, and dedicated her life to the emancipation movement and the welfare of others.

Allow for Differences in Sensing and Intuition in Wording of Questions

Mary McCaulley, Ph.D., psychology professor and colleague of Isabel Myers, reported that "Isabel had us making tests for different preferences. We had to have enough questions so that everyone had to answer some from each preference. But we had extra questions so you could choose which ones to skip."[2] Not a bad idea and not difficult to implement. This approach also incorporates the motivation generated for students by giving them a choice.

In our experience, the critical place to begin to engage students in order for them to perceive accurately the questions being asked is with the perceiving functions of Sensing and Intuition.

A Reminder

- *Sensing* focuses on practical applications, what, and how

- *Intuition* focuses on theory, meaning, and possibilities

- *Sensing* responds to a step-by-step approach

- *Intuition* responds to the big picture

- *Sensing* uses realistic specifics about what is known

- *Intuition* uses imagination and hunches

Teachers Ivan and Sharon were so struck by their own differences that they began mutual consultation on preparing test questions. They continued to consult with each other when they shared common objectives in order to provide questions phrased in both Sensing and Intuitive language.

Additional Examples of Balancing Sensing and Intuition

In the exercise shown in Example 1, students were asked to demonstrate the ability to write effectively with a clear understanding of the standards of composition involved.

Example 1

Option 1 (INTUITION)	**Option 2 (SENSING)**
Rank your pieces of writing in order of most to least effective with a rationale for what you think are the good and bad points of each. What did you learn from that particular assignment? Think about why your best piece of writing is your best piece. Talk about the standards you were supposed to reach in a particular piece. Did you reach them? Talk about the process you went through for a particular piece and how that developed into your favorite piece. Be as specific as you can.	1. Rank your pieces of writing in order of most to least effective. 2. Give a rationale for what you think the good and bad points of each are. 3. Tell what you learned from each assignment. 4. Explain why your best piece of writing is your best. 5. Select one piece of your work and write about the standards you were supposed to reach and if you reached them. 6. Select another piece and write about the process you went through to write it. Tell how the piece developed into a favorite or less-favorite piece.

In the second example, Sharon (who preferred Sensing) reported that the phrase "reflect on" wasn't clear to her and also that she wanted to know sooner what she was *to do* with the question.

Example 2

Option 1 (INTUITION)	**Option 2 (SENSING)**
In the first act and scene of *Macbeth*, the witches make the statement, "Fair is foul and foul is fair; Hover through the fog and filthy air." Reflect on how this statement becomes a theme for the play. Who echoes this statement later on in the first act? How does this statement reflect *Macbeth*'s character? How does this passage relate to our lives today? Be specific.	Give some examples from *Macbeth* where the theme, "Fair is foul and foul is fair: Hover through the fog and filthy air," is repeated. How does this statement become a theme for the play? How does this statement reflect *Macbeth*'s character? How does this passage relate to our lives today?

A middle school science teacher with a preference for Sensing consulted with a colleague to develop assessment questions. He asked a fellow teacher with a preference for Intuition how to best elicit from his Intuitive students their understanding of the nature of ecosystems. The collaborative results are detailed in example 3.

Example 3

Option 1 (INTUITION)	Option 2 (SENSING)
Explain the underlying principles of ecosystems. Select an ecosystem occurring in this state and suggest a policy that addresses concerns regarding the ecosystem's most vulnerable components. Explain where the intervention should occur and describe the resulting effect on the components of the system.	1. Choose an ecosystem that occurs in this state. Identify and define the components of this system. 2. Explain the interaction between each of these components. 3. Based on what is known to have occurred in the last three decades in the system, identify the two most vulnerable components and give your reasons for these choices. 4. Introduce a change in the system that would have impact on one of these vulnerable components. Make a graph to illustrate the stages of change that would occur throughout the system.

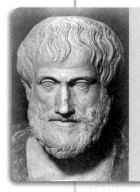

GREAT MINDS

"Education is an ornament in prosperity and a refuge in adversity."

ARISTOTLE (384–322 B.C.) A Greek philosopher and natural scientist who wrote on subjects ranging from heavenly bodies to biology to ethics and politics. He deeply influenced later thinkers who used his insights to help systematize the study of the world.

You will see that both choices involve students in factual recall, analysis, and problem solving—all of which involve both basic knowledge and critical thinking. While both break the assignment into steps, the directions suggested by the Intuitive teacher are more open-ended with fewer precise parameters such as "last three decades" or "two most." The difference here has to do with engagement of the student with the assignment. The more specified guidelines that clarify statements for Sensing tend to inhibit Intuition. Would it make a difference to you which question was on your test? Would you like to be given the option to select between the two questions?

Another strategy for developing questions to engage students with type differences is to construct a template that can be used as a reference and framework when developing test questions. Figure 4.1 shows such a framework. Students can be asked to answer at least some of the questions from each side.

These same questions can be converted to multiple-choice questions as shown in figure 4.2 (page 76).

NOTE: *this table and the ones following return to the typical configuration of S–N, rather than N–S.*

Figure 4.1 *Sensing and Intuition Questions: Short Answer*

Sensing (S)	Intuition (N)
Give a definition for _____.	What is the major difference between _____ and _____?
Use the word _____ in a sentence.	What is an antonym for _____?
Give an example of substance that can be formed using the elements _____ _____.	Using only the elements in _____, change the formula to produce two other substances.

RESOURCES

These templates are available in reproducible form in **RESOURCE 13**, *Test Questions: Differences for Sensing and Intuition.*

Figure 4.2 *Sensing and Intuition Questions: Multiple Choice*

Sensing (S)	Intuition (N)
The best definition for _____ is: a. _____ b. _____ c. _____ Which of the following sentences uses the word _____ correctly? a. _____ b. _____ c. _____ Which of the following substances can be formed from the correct amounts of _____, _____, and _____? a. _____ b. _____ c. _____	What is the major difference between _____ and _____? a. _____ b. _____ c. _____ Which of the following is an antonym for _____? a. _____ b. _____ c. _____ Which of the following substances represents a correct combination of the same elements formed in _____? a. _____ b. _____ c. _____

Standardized Testing

Standardized tests are a fact of life for students, and the stakes are high. Final exams in high school classes are supplemented with standardized end-of-course tests, and the results are factored in as a high percentage of the course grade. More states are requiring exit exams that seniors must pass before graduation. Students at all levels must pass end-of-grade tests in order to be promoted to the next grade. Students need to be able to understand the test questions and understand them quickly on a timed test.

Type Differences in Testing Performance

Research correlating MBTI types with standardized tests indicate that while differences are not great, there are clear trends in how well students with a preference for Sensing performed on standardized tests compared to students with a preference for Intuition.[3] In general, while there are always individual exceptions, groups of students with a preference for Intuition do as well or better on tests of *aptitude* than groups of students with a preference for Sensing. Conversely, groups of students with a preference for Sensing do as well or better than groups of students with a preference for Intuition on tests of *achievement*—again recognizing that there are many individual exceptions.

Even if not large, trends that are this apparent merit attention when we are looking for tools to help individual students achieve their highest potential. Type theory suggests that there may be several reasons for these differences in performance that are explainable by psychological type.

Timed Tests

Most tests of aptitude are *timed* assessments, a reality that works to the disadvantage of many students with a preference for Sensing. The Sensing function is concerned with specificity, so people with a preference for Sensing are very conscientious about understanding each specific word, phrase, and sentence. When asked how they read a book, they generally reply they read every word on every page. On the other hand, when people with a preference for Intuition are asked the same question, they often reveal that while there are some books they read cover to cover, there are others that they read enough of to get the general gist, or they only skim sections of a book that may not interest them very much. Yet they still report that they've "read" the book.[4]

This same dynamic often applies to the way people with preferences for Sensing and Intuition differ in how they take multiple-choice tests—the most frequent format for standardized testing. Sensing types read questions and alternative answers more slowly, often rereading them more than once to make sure they understand each word clearly. It simply takes them more time to answer the questions than it does Intuitive types who read the questions and answers quickly and more often trust their "gut feeling" about which answer is correct. They thus tend to get more questions answered. The *disadvantage* of this practice for students preferring Intuition is that they often miss specifics, including crucial words in the questions such as the qualifiers "always" or "usually."

Isabel Myers described the test-taking mindsets between Sensing and Intuition as "soundness of understanding (vs.) quickness of understanding."[5] This soundness, of course, is a basic strength of Sensing, something that emphasis on speed dilutes. Myers recommends that teachers not put time limits on their own tests so that Sensing students are permitted "to demonstrate their ability without having to violate their principle of making sure. By taking the time limit off the tests, teachers could turn them into power tests instead of speed tests."[6]

Type Differences in Test Questions

If teachers recognize how questions require differing uses of the four functions, they can then help individual students "decode" questions that are unclear to them and make more intentional use of their less preferred function. Four examples of these differences follow—two from a standardized math test and two from a standardized biology test.

The following two examples are sample questions for an end-of-course exam given to Algebra I students in one state. Both questions require the use of analysis and logic (i.e., the Thinking function) but differ in their use of Sensing and Intuition.

*Question 1 (Sensing and Thinking)**

$$\text{Simplify:} \quad \frac{14c^3d^2 - 21c^2d^3}{14cd^2}$$

This problem is fairly straight forward. To answer this, the student follows the rules learned for working with algebraic equations.

*Question 2 (Intuition and Thinking)**
A rectangular pen has a length 3 feet greater than its width. If both dimensions are increased by 5 feet, which expression gives the resulting increase in area?

    a. $10x + 40$
    b. $13x + 40$
    c. $x^2 + 13x + 40$
    d. $x^2 + 10x + 40$

To answer this question a student must now translate words which are symbols themselves into other symbols and then deal with unknowns in addition to the known rules of algebra. (Sounds compli-

*Released sample EOC item used by permission of the North Carolina Department of Public Instruction.

cated to us!) The student must find a formula to calculate the area of a rectangular pen when the width and length are unknowns.

To deconstruct this abstract-sounding problem, the student can engage Sensing with a visual diagram of a rectangle, use what he has learned about solving problems, and represent the unknown width with X and the unknown length with X + 3.

The student would use the following steps to solve the problem:

1. Recall that the formula for finding the area of a rectangle is length times width.

2. Draw a diagram to represent the rectangle. The length is X + 3 and the width is X.

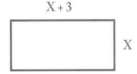

The equation that represents the area of the original rectangle is $X(X+3)$

3. Increase both the length and width by 5.

The length of this rectangle is X+ 3 + 5 and the width is X + 5. The length is thus X + 8 and the width is X+ 5.

4. Draw a diagram to represent the rectangle. The length is X + 3 + 5 and the width is X+5.

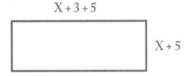

The equation that represents the area of the rectangle when the dimensions are increased by 5 feet is: $(X + 8)(X + 5)$.

The question asks us to find the expression that gives us the increase in area when both dimensions are increased by 5 feet.

5. We will need to subtract the area of the original rectangle from the area of the rectangle when the dimensions are increased by 5 feet.

This expression is $(X + 8)(X + 5) - X(X + 3)$ which simplifies to $(X^2 + 13X + 40) - (X^2 + 3X) = 10X + 40$.

The correct answer then is (a).

We have turned the question into a straight forward math problem rather than something abstract. Even young Intuitive types can benefit from learning how to "deconstruct" a conceptual question into its component parts or use visuals to make concrete a problem presented through the symbols known as words.

Two examples from a high school biology end-of-course exam:

Question 1*

Which of the following is found only in eukaryotic cells?

    A. cell membrane

    B. cytoplasm

    C. DNA

    D. Mitochondria

Question 2*

A plant has been removed from its natural environment and placed into a body of water that contains more salt than the inside of each plant cell. This situation is **most similar** to which of the following events?

    A. a sea plant put into fresh water

    B. a freshwater plant put into sea water

    C. a sea plant put into distilled water

    D. a land plant put into tap water

Question 1 requires recall of factual data and employs Sensing. *Question 2* requires factual knowledge as well but also requires taking several sets of factual knowledge and determining the commonalities and differences and comparing relationships. Intuition is used to decipher the word symbols combined with the logical analysis of Thinking. (The correct answers are 1D and 2B.)

So what are some of the implications of these Sensing and Intuition differences for helping students of different types learn to perform best on timed multiple-choice tests? Students who prefer Sensing can be taught to read the questions and answers carefully, eliminating answers they know to be wrong. Then they can reread and think about the remaining answers and can learn to trust their instincts more when deciding between them.

Students with a preference for Intuition can be encouraged to read *every* word, perhaps using their pencil to point to each word as they read, being particularly careful to note the qualifiers such as "always" and "never."

All students, but particularly those with a preference for Intuition, can be taught to break complex-sounding problems into steps, using visual diagramming when possible. These and other suggestions are laid out in user-friendly fashion by Judith Provost in her book *Strategies for Success: Using Type to Do Better in High School and College.*

*Released sample EOC item used by permission of the North Carolina Department of Public Instruction.

In our experience, the place to begin to accommodate differences in test-taking is to focus on recognizing the differences between a question that primarily engages Sensing and a question that primarily engages Intuition. Sensing and Intuition understand things differently because the functions pay attention to different information.

Additionally, most standardized test questions also ask students to engage their function of Thinking (combined with Sensing or Intuition) and to a lesser degree the function of Feeling. Sometimes both are engaged, usually with different questions. The following are examples of middle school reading comprehension questions.

THE STUMP
By Donald Hall

Today they cut down the oak.
Strong men climbed with ropes
In the brittle tree.
The exhaust of a gasoline saw
Was blue in the branches.

It is February. The oak has been dead a year.
I remember the great sails of its branches
Rolling out greenly, a hundred and twenty feet up,
And acorns thick on the lawn.
Nine cities of squirrels lived in that tree.
Today they run over the snow
Squeaking their lamentation.

Yet I was happy that it was coming down
"Let it come down!" I kept saying to myself
With a joy that was strange to me.
Though the oak was the shade of old summers,
I loved the guttural saw.

From "The Stump," OLD AND NEW POEMS. Copyright 1990 by Donald Hall.
Reprinted by permission of Ticknor & Fields/Houghton Mifflin Co. All rights reserved.

*After you read the poem, review the following two questions:**

Question 1

Which of the following lines from the poem *does not* show an important contrast?

    A. Strong men climbed with ropes / in the brittle tree.

    B. It is February. The oak has been dead a year.

    C. Nine cities of squirrels lived in that tree. / Today they run over the snow.

    D. "Let it come down!" I kept saying to myself / With a joy that was strange to me.

(Correct answer is B.)

Question 2

What are the mixed emotions of the character in this poem? Explain.

_____

_____

_____

    Both questions require the use of the Thinking and Feeling functions, yet there is an emphasis on one or the other of these two functions in each question.

Question 1: While analytical thinking is required for most of this question, option D still requires some Feeling judgment with regard to the "joy that was strange to me."

Question 2: Ability to infer the personal values (Feeling) of the poet is a prerequisite for answering the question. Yet a thorough answer also requires the inclusion of a clear, logical, well-developed explanation (Thinking) which references the poem.

*Released sample EOG item used by permission of the North Carolina Department of Public Instruction.

GREAT MINDS

"I am turned into a sort of machine for observing facts and grinding out conclusions."

CHARLES DARWIN (1809–1882) The English naturalist outlined his theory of natural selection as the driving force behind evolutionary biology. His book, *On The Origin of Species,* revolutionized the explanatory power of biology and shook the culture of the times with its challenge to biblical notions of creation.

Ideally, students who know type can learn to recognize when questions require them to use their less-preferred processes and become aware of the extra attention these answers may need. At the very least, teachers can make sure students have ample opportunity to work in class with questions that make use of all four mental processes of Sensing, Intuition, Thinking, and Feeling.

Taking College Entrance Exams

One of the authors, Sondra, made use of these Sensing and Intuition differences while counseling high school students taking college entrance exams. The two major tests accepted by colleges and universities are the SAT® and the ACT.® The SAT is primarily a test of scholastic *aptitude* requiring the use of inferential skills that employ Intuition. The ACT is primarily a test of what has actually been learned, which employs the Sensing function. So while some students do well no matter which type of test they are taking, Sondra encouraged students who were more marginal in their ability to do well to take *both* the SAT and ACT and submit whichever score was higher. She found that often students with a preference for Sensing performed better on the ACT than the SAT with the reverse true for students with a preference for Intuition. Interestingly, though they may not know the differences between Sensing and Intuition, similar advice has been given by some school counselors who recognize that students differ on how they perform on the two assessments.[7] One can only conjecture that type differences may play a part.

Type and GPA

Studies shows that among large groups of high school students, scholastic aptitude scores correlate with academic achievement as measured by grade point averages (GPA) for all the types. However, for each pair of types that share the same first three preferences (for example ESTJ and ESTP), the students with a preference for Judging in that pair have higher GPAs as a group than their counterparts with a preference for Perceiving.[8] This is consistent with type theory since students with a Judging preference usually organize their lives and work, plan their work with a deadline in view, are bothered by lack of closure, and turn their completed work in on time.

On the other hand, students with a preference for Perceiving score as a group higher on scholastic aptitude measures than their Judging counterparts.

Individuals, of course, may differ from these patterns. Several hypotheses have been put forward to explain these differences in scores. The Perceiving attitude is more focused on process than closure and manages time with a view toward postponing completion until a deadline. Sometimes assignments may remain incomplete past the deadline. Others have suggested that the Perceiving attitude produces a sense of curiosity that leads students with this preference into many directions which distracts from completion of one particular assignment. This curiosity in young people may also foster varied interests and life experiences that aid students with the questions on standardized tests.

To Wrap It Up

We strongly believe type makes a difference in how students are best able to *demonstrate* their learning as well as how they *attain* their learning. In the words of McTighe and O'Conner in their writing about assessment, "To make valid inferences about learning, teachers need to allow students to work to their strengths."[9] In an ideal world, students who know type can learn to recognize when assessment questions require them to use their less-preferred processes, and they can become aware of the extra attention the selection of these answers may need. At the very least, teachers can make sure students have ample opportunity to work in class with assessments of all kinds that allow them to make use of all four mental processes of Sensing, Intuition, Thinking, and Feeling.

Personalizing assessment, while presenting a teacher with new challenges, offers the rewards of greater motivation, higher achievement, greater self-concepts, and fewer discipline problems. It's not a bad investment!

In a Nutshell

- Teaching students to engage in ongoing self-assessment based on type produces better outcomes for their assignments or portfolios as well as teaching students life skills for their future workplaces.
- More emphasis on personalized assessment enables students to have a greater opportunity to demonstrate what they know.
- The Perceiving preferences of Sensing and Intuition understand things differently, so these two mental functions are a critical consideration in designing test questions.
- Timed tests can work to the disadvantage of Sensing types who are very conscientious about understanding each specific word, phrase, and sentence and, therefore, typically take more time to read and answer test questions.

- Students with a preference for Intuition typically read sentences for the general idea and trust their hunches about the answers. They may often miss the specifics, including crucial words in test questions.

- Students who know type can learn to recognize when assessments require them to use their less-preferred mental processes and become aware of the extra attention these items may need.

Check Your Understanding

Q *The following two questions assess the same knowledge but are asked in two different ways. Which of the two questions is likely to stimulate a good response from (a) Sensing and (b) Intuition?*

Question 1
Compare modern controversies related to powers of the U.S. government to the debates between Federalists and Anti-Federalists over adoption of the U.S. Constitution.

Question 2
a. Identify at least three issues that the Federalists and Anti-Federalists debated before adopting the U.S. Constitution.

b. Identify issues debated today concerning states' rights vs. federal power

c. Describe how these two sets of issues (a and b) are similar.

A *Those who prefer Intuition will likely relate well to question 1. The narrative and more open-ended question leave the impression of many possibilities to be considered—a stimulus for Intuition. Discussing how seemingly disconnected things might relate also appeals to Intuition.*

Those who prefer Sensing will likely relate well to question 2. The question is broken into parts and listed in step-by-step fashion that more easily engages the Sensing function. The use of bullets, words such as "identify," and the parameter of "at least 3 issues" leave the impression of something specific that stimulates Sensing.

Q *Self-assessment is an important skill to learn. The most thorough assessment includes use of all four of the mental functions of Sensing, Intuition, Thinking, and Feeling. Each of the following groups is related to one of these functions.*

Can you match each group with its function?

A. Am I considering all possible options?
   Are there any patterns or themes?
   What is the big picture of what I want to accomplish?
   Where else can I apply what I've learned?

B. Why did I decide on this project?
   Do the facts support my strategies?
   Am I following a logical order?
   If my project worked well, what led to its success?

C. What is most important to me about this project?
   What personal meaning will I get from this work?
   Am I giving this project appropriate effort?
   How satisfied am I with my finished product?

D. What specifically do the instructions say?
   What do I already know about this?
   What else do I need to know and what materials do I need?
   What is the step-by-step way to approach this project?

A *Group A: Intuition; Group B: Thinking; Group C: Feeling; Group D: Sensing.*

Getting Started

- Review one of your recent quizzes or tests. Evaluate which preferences (Sensing, Intuition, Thinking, Feeling) are likely to be stimulated with the questions.

- Select three questions from the quiz or test. Write each of these questions in a form likely to stimulate Sensing and a form likely to stimulate Intuition. The template found in Resource 13 can help with this process.

- Consult with a colleague of a different type to develop test questions and find alternative ways to assess students' knowledge.

Personalizing Pathways to Achievement

We do not teach the brain to think. We can, however, help learners to organize content to facilitate more complex processing.

DAVID SOUSA, M.D., *How the Brain Learns*

Education professor Gordon Lawrence believes achievement is a by-product of type development. He proposes that if the goal is to bring about fundamental change in the structure of schools, then priority must be given to type development—not simply attention to learning styles.[1]

One of Isabel Myers' major contributions to Jung's theory of personality type is her emphasis on the crucial nature of good type development for a person to function effectively in all areas, including learning. Jung wrote little about type development as a *system* of development yet gave clear indication that there is a hierarchy of development for each of the types[2]—indeed he indicated that it is not appropriate for all of the functions to develop at once. Drawing from his scattered comments about the relationship between the four functions, Myers inferred from Jung a natural and unique path of development of these functions for each of the types.

The natural paths of type development for all sixteen types are illustrated in table 5.a. The small letter following each function designates whether that function is more often in the Extraverted or Introverted attitude.

Early Development of Type

As youngsters we use all four functions in an immature state, but when we begin to make conscious decisions, brain hard wiring leads us to rely on one of the four as the predominant function in our minds. Unless frustrated by environmental

Table 5.a *Order of Type Preferences*

ISTJ	ISFJ	INFJ	INTJ
1. Sensing (i)	1. Sensing (i)	1. Intuition (i)	1. Intuition (i)
2. Thinking (e)	2. Feeling (e)	2. Feeling (e)	2. Thinking (e)
3. Feeling (e)	3. Thinking (e)	3. Thinking (e)	3. Feeling (e)
4. Intuition (e)	4. Intuition (e)	4. Sensing (e)	4. Sensing (e)
ISTP	**ISFP**	**INFP**	**INTP**
1. Thinking (i)	1. Feeling (i)	1. Feeling (i)	1. Thinking (i)
2. Sensing (e)	2. Sensing (e)	2. Intuition (e)	2. Intuition (e)
3. Intuition (e)	3. Intuition (e)	3. Sensing (e)	3. Sensing (e)
4. Feeling (e)	4. Thinking (e)	4. Thinking (e)	4. Feeling (e)
ESTP	**ESFP**	**ENFP**	**ENTP**
1. Sensing (e)	1. Sensing (e)	1. Intuition (e)	1. Intuition (e)
2. Thinking (i)	2. Feeling (i)	2. Feeling (i)	2. Thinking (i)
3. Feeling (i)	3. Thinking (i)	3. Thinking (i)	3. Feeling (i)
4. Intuition (i)	4. Intuition (i)	4. Sensing (i)	4. Sensing (i)
ESTJ	**ESFJ**	**ENFJ**	**ENTJ**
1. Thinking (e)	1. Feeling (e)	1. Feeling (e)	1. Thinking (e)
2. Sensing (i)	2. Sensing (i)	2. Intuition (i)	2. Intuition (i)
3. Intuition (i)	3. Intuition (i)	3. Sensing (i)	3. Sensing (i)
4. Feeling (i)	4. Thinking (i)	4. Thinking (i)	4. Feeling (i)

factors, sometime early in childhood this function begins to differentiate or separate from the other functions and becomes the most relied on, the most practiced, the most trustworthy, and the most dominant of the four functions for the rest of the person's life. Typically, this function is used most often in the direction of a person's preference for either Extraversion or Introversion.

This process of type development is rather like a young child learning about and playing four different sports and then finding one of them more interesting and perhaps more natural to his or her body. So the child practices and plays this sport *more* often than the others.

For instance, if the dominant function for an *Extraverted* child is Sensing, from an early age that child will likely touch and manipulate everything in sight, moving from one thing to another, energetically gathering information through the senses. This behavior may be so consistent that the child may be called hyperactive by some people. If the dominant function for an *Introverted* child is Sensing, that child will observe many things through sight and sound and file these facts away mentally, but this gathering of data may be undetected by others so the child is likely to be called shy by some people.

When later, a second function begins to emerge and pair up with the dominant function in a supportive role, the behavior of both children typically becomes more balanced. For the Extraverted child, this second function is usually experienced in the Introverted attitude, so the Extraverted Sensing child who may have been seen as hyperactive begins to set priorities through Introverted use of either Thinking or Feeling judgment. This child may channel the Sensing experiences into focused activities with others who share an enjoyment of fun-loving activities such as sports or physically-demanding work. For the Introverted child, this second function is usually experienced in the Extraverted attitude, so the Introverted Sensing child who had been seen as shy may begin to apply that inner storehouse of data either by finding tactile activities to share with close friends or by doing tasks such as organizing personal collections or databases.

Dominant and Auxiliary Functions

In the language of personality type, the first function in the hierarchy is known as the *dominant* function. The supportive second function is called the *auxiliary*.

Inclusion of Extraversion and Introversion

The dominant function is used most often in the preferred attitude of Extraversion or Introversion and the remaining functions are in the opposite. Thus, Extraverts more typically extravert their dominant function and introvert their auxiliary function. The reverse is true for an Introvert. For example:

ESTJ	ISTJ
Dominant function Thinking (Extraverted)	Dominant function Sensing (Introverted)
Auxiliary function Sensing (Introverted)	Auxiliary function Thinking (Extraverted)

The hierarchy for these two types suggests the following: young ESTJ types who extravert their dominant thinking function are likely to state their opinions on matters very early in life in direct ways even if they do not have adequate factual data to back them up. Young ISTJ types who introvert their dominant sensing function are likely to possess a wealth of information they've observed, but unless asked, others may be totally unaware of this. As these types mature into early adolescence and beyond, the ESTJ types will build a better factual base for their decisions. People will still hear their opinions, but when challenged, they will be able to back up their judgments with data and their school work is likely to reflect this. Their dominant function will continue to lead them to take charge of many things, but this leadership will be more responsible. The ISTJ types will find more outlets for their interest in data. They may gravitate toward technical subjects and be interested in practical applications in the world around them with their dominant function continuing to lead them to precision and thoroughness.

Inclusion of Perception and Judgment

You'll notice that for both the Extravert and Introvert, one of these first two functions is a perception function and the other is a judgment function. This inclusion of both perception and judgment explains why there is better balance as the second function develops and the individual has a more sound way of perceiving *and* of making judgments. This balance of perception and judgment comprises what it takes for more mature decisions. Continuing with our sports analogy, this would be like adding another sport from your original four that you would practice as well. However, the first sport would remain your favorite and still receive most of your energy and attention.

GREAT MINDS

"I was obliged to be industrious; whoever is equally industrious will succeed equally well."

JOHANN SEBASTIAN BACH (1685–1750) This German composer is often ranked as among the greatest musical minds. His synthesis of Baroque musical styles is complex enough to confound the casual listener, but works such as his cello suites provide endless fascination to serious students of music.

Later Development of Type

The remaining two functions get some development during the school years, but for most people these come into conscious use in the personality during the adult years. The third function in the hierarchy is called the *tertiary* function and the fourth is called the *inferior* or sometimes the *least-preferred* function. As the first and second functions develop and engage the conscious energy of a person, these third and fourth functions hang out more in the unconscious, sort of like waiting their turn—though they do make conscious appearances when called into service intentionally. Using our previous example:

ESTJ	ISTJ
Dominant function Thinking (Extraverted)	Dominant function Sensing (Introverted)
Auxiliary function Sensing (Introverted)	Auxiliary function Thinking (Extraverted)
Tertiary function Intuition (Introverted)	Tertiary function Feeling (Extraverted)
Inferior function Feeling (Introverted)	Inferior function Intuition (Extraverted)

These hierarchies suggest that both ESTJ and ISTJ types will be more task focused early in life and be interested in activities that rely on organization and consistency rather than new ideas or personal concerns of people. Their sensitivity to others and willingness to experiment with innovation typically develops later in life.

There is no time-table template for development of these functions as that depends on individual life circumstances. Sometimes the functions that are hard-wired to be first or second in the personality get discounted or are not engaged by a person's early environment and do not develop until later in adulthood. The hierarchy of the functions within each type often factor into career choices. Many an adult has gone into a job because of the expectations of others, felt mismatched with their work interests, and later made a major career change stating that "I am finally doing what I always wanted to do." The smoother career path is more likely to take place when there is a match between early career choices and the dominant and auxiliary functions. Later a person may desire to make a change by adding work or personal activities that engage more of the third and fourth functions. These people often say, "I'm making life more interesting with this change and building on what I did earlier."

Again using the sports analogy, we would say that it is like finding the two remaining of those four sports tried as a child interesting after all—first one and then the other—and deciding that rather than being a one-or two-sport person, you will become more of an all-round athlete later in life. While it might be somewhat awkward for you to learn the sports you had only dabbled in as a youngster, the effort holds a fascination for you and makes life interesting as you build new skills. Actually, to frame this analogy in a true Jungian mode, those third and fourth functions may demand your attention in some way if they are ignored in mid-to late adulthood, sometimes in dreams—perhaps having nightmares of finding yourself on the playing field of one of those two sports with thousands watching and you suddenly realize you don't know how to play![3]

School Is Important for Type Development

In an ideal world, along with home and other environmental influences, pre-school and elementary school are fertile environments for children to develop their dominant functions. Hence it is critical for teachers to develop learning activities and assessments and create learning environments that make it possible for this natural development to occur. Referring again to the handedness analogy mentioned previously in this book, not allowing the natural dominant function to develop through use and practice would be like not providing left-handed students with appropriate desks and scissors and not allowing them to write with their left hand.

Often, the second function gets more use and practice with the more complex decision making required in middle and high school. Then by the time the young adult goes out into the real world he or she has a mind equipped with a well-developed perception function and a well-developed judgment function to gather and process information for adult decisions.

Given choices, students most often develop in accordance with their natural patterns. Following one's hardwired pathway to development of the four functions does not have to be forced—a person simply needs to be given opportunity to follow their type's pathway in their unique way. Schools can create structures in which this development is able to occur.

Helping Underachieving Students Develop Strengths

Teachers play the role of skilled diagnosticians every day as they search for ways to reach their students. Certainly, type issues warrant exploring even though they do not always explain the reason for students' lack of success. Sometimes a negative emotional interference is the main reason students get off track, often triggered by what is happening at home or elsewhere. It is important for teachers to ask about home situations that could be interfering with learning and acknowledge these difficulties with understanding and assistance when appropriate.

All types also can have negative emotional reactions that can get them off track when their classroom experiences do not allow them to use their dominant and auxiliary functions. When teachers have eliminated other reasons students are not achieving at optimum levels, they can then turn to type as an intervention. This can provide students with the opportunity to connect to their natural strengths through their dominant and auxiliary functions. Often, this strategy will help them get back on track.

The first four chapters of this book provided options for helping students access their dominant and auxiliary functions once they are identified. Often, teachers must *estimate* a student's type, and so behavior cues such as the following can be helpful for determining which interventions to try.

Sensing Types

- Remember facts and specifics.
- Speak concisely.
- Seek visual, auditory, and tactile stimuli.
- Often finds ways to do something physically active in the moment, particularly when there is a preference for Extraversion.
- Are often alert to the specific aspects of things going on in the class but reveal this only if asked, particularly when there is a preference for Introversion.
- Are more engaged when a task requires skills already learned.
- Respond better to clear, sequential directions than to more open-ended guidelines.

Intuitive Types

- Like to try out, talk, or think about new ideas simply because they are new.
- Talk more in big picture or conceptual generalities.
- Facts and specifics tend to elude them.
- Engage in a lot of imagination and fantasy.
- Tend to make up their own directions rather than follow those given.
- Are more excited about a task or idea when they approach it creatively.

Thinking Types

- Like to problem solve and single-mindedly focus on a problem until it is solved.
- Show more interest in things, actions, or ideas than people and their feelings.
- Frequently ask, "Why?" and want an answer that is logical.
- Question the opinions of others.
- Selectively offer praise to others.
- Are stimulated by competition.

Feeling Types

- Look for opportunities to be social, even if with only one or two others.
- Are alert to other people's feelings.
- Show a caring attitude.
- Are often conciliatory in conflict situations.
- Show passion about what matters to them.
- Offer appreciation and praise freely.

Type and Intelligence

This is a good place to say a word about the difference between *intelligence* and type. We subscribe to the theory that there are different kinds of intelligences, all involving cognitive processes.[4] According to this theory, individuals vary in the aptitude they possess for each kind of intelligence, no one having the same level of aptitude or competence with them all. In our complex world, this evolutionary, adaptive phenomenon serves society well. Type, we believe, explains how a person takes in and processes the information required for use within each of the forms of intelligences. Myers went so far as to conclude that "within limits, type development can substitute for intelligence, because average intelligence fully utilized through fine type development, will give results far above expectation. However a serious deficit of type development, especially a deficit of judgment, constitutes a disability for which no amount of intelligence can compensate."[5]

Type development means that students begin to differentiate the functions into the hierarchy of development intended by their brain's hardwiring. Myers' own research with students of all ages showed a significant effect of type preferences on learning, beginning with how *not* teaching children to learn to decode "sound-symbols" of words put Sensing children at a distinct disadvantage as soon as reading was introduced, especially those with Extraverted Sensing.[6]

94   GREAT MINDS DON'T THINK ALIKE

Since then, numerous studies have been conducted on the impact of type on learning[7] with results indicating a strong positive correlation between achievement and clarity of a student's preferred ways of perception and judgment.

The practical question, of course, is how can schools foster development of type so that students can achieve, whatever their kind or kinds of intelligence?

Teachers Can Begin with Personalized Instruction

Teachers can intentionally vary learning activities to include the four mental functions of Sensing, Intuition, Thinking, and Feeling and intentionally develop a vocabulary of words for instruction that engages each of these functions—especially Sensing and Intuition.

When a teacher's type preferences are the same as a student's, the teacher is likely to emphasize and engage the best mental gifts of that student. The danger comes when the teacher's preferences and emphases are different from the student's and the student is told "Do your best work!" with the expectation that the student will use his or her mind the same way as the teacher does. Not only does the student in this case have to work much harder to achieve the same goals, but he or she also may not develop a way of perception and judgment that feels natural and trustworthy.

Likewise, it is important that the teacher be aware of the importance of using all four functions and be willing to assist students with the development of their less-preferred ways of perception and judgment. When teacher and students share the same preferences, they may also share the same blind spots.

General Guidelines to Promote Type Development in the Classroom

Teachers have numerous opportunities for fostering good type development. They can ask students how they learn best, build student capacity, help students set goals, include students in lesson planning, offer students choices of learning activities and include opportunities for community responsibilities.

Ask Students How They Learn Best

At the beginning of each term give students a chance to tell you how they learn best. The direct benefit of this exercise is to gain information about the learning preferences for each student that can be used if any of these students begin to "fall through the cracks." The indirect benefit is the message you give students that you see and care about them as individuals and will treat them accordingly.

RESOURCES

RESOURCE 17, *To Do My Best Work I Need . . .*, can be used to gather this information.

This practice also makes students aware of how they best take in information and process it for decisions, helping them become more self-reliant for their own learning. The technical language of type does not have to be used to explain the concepts. The point is to let students know that the different ways minds are engaged are all equally valuable—that people just find some ways more natural than others, and it is helpful for individuals to figure out their most natural ways.

Build Student Capacity

Emphasize the expectation that students not only can but also *will* find satisfaction from competence. Make it clear to students *explicitly* that they can do the work and help them believe this by making it possible to work utilizing their preferred mental functions. (See chapter 2 on personalizing learning.) Make it clear to students *implicitly* by insisting that a certain level of accomplishment must be achieved in order for the course or task to be completed. Implicit in this expectation is the belief that the student has the capacity to reach an acceptable level of competence.

Frequently ask questions, such as the following, to engage each mental function.

Sensing

- What do you already know about this?
- What evidence do you have for your thoughts?
- What do you observe?

Intuition

- What other ideas does this suggest to you?
- What do your hunches tell you?
- What insights do you have about this?
- How can you add your own creativity to this?

Thinking

- What do you think the outcome will be if you do that?
- What is the most logical thing to say (or do)?
- How would you work on solving that logically?
- How would you analyze that situation?

Feeling

- How do you think your idea will affect people?
- What does this mean to you personally?
- How can you help your team members?
- What is most important to you about this?

Help Students Set Goals

At the beginning of the school year or course, ask students to determine their goals for themselves in your class and make a note of these. Ask as well, "What do you need to accomplish these goals?" Listen for students expressing type preferences. If students know type, use type labels; if they do not, use the concepts the labels represent and ask students to consider goals related to missing functions. For instance, the teacher might ask "How would you include more factual data (S), imagination (N), objectivity (T), personal meaning (F) into your work?"

When students want to improve something specific, e.g., their writing, they may be encouraged to develop specific goals for each of the functions. For example:

- I want to be more careful with grammar (Sensing).
- I want to use more of my imagination (Intuition).
- I want to use more critical analysis (Thinking).
- I want to reflect more of what matters to me personally (Feeling).

Remember to ask students, "How will you accomplish this?"

Part of the goal setting process should include a specified time when the student and teacher evaluate the goals. This becomes a time for celebration or modification as needed.

Include Students in Lesson Planning

From time to time, explain your own natural way of learning and acknowledge that you understand that people learn best in different ways. Occasionally try out the question, "If this is our learning objective, what strategy would you use to make this lesson best for you?" Encourage clarifying questions on the part of students if they do not understand the instructions. Students must correctly perceive an assignment before they can carry it out. Let them know you recognize there are different ways to say the same thing and that you are aware you may not be saying it in the best way for them.

Check with students regarding the time you allow for an assignment. Give them permission to say if things are moving either too quickly or too slowly. Negotiate a reasonable time with the group then plan for any individual exceptions.

Offer Choices in Learning Activities

If you offer students choices for learning activities that you have based on type groupings, note or keep a record of the groupings each student selects. When you notice a student choosing selections from the same grouping, encourage them to "experiment" with an activity from another grouping. Be especially alert in ongoing assessments to urge students to ask themselves questions that engage all the preferences.

RESOURCES

RESOURCE 14, *Student Self-Assessment*, provides a list of such questions students can use.

Include Opportunities for Community Responsibilities

Allow students to choose an area of community responsibility for what goes on in the classroom. Sometimes students will select tasks that use their preferred mental functions and there likely will be obvious reasons to praise them. If a task proves to be unsatisfactory to a student, the teacher can evaluate the situation to determine if there is possibly a type-based reason, and discuss this with the student. The art of such a discussion, of course, is not to devalue or discourage the student's use of less-preferred functions but to recognize that some tasks may be more interesting and natural. The student has a choice as to whether to make a selection based on what is natural or to choose a task that offers the challenge of stretching his or her mind.

Our data collection from workshops we've conducted with students produced the following choices for preferred community responsibilities.

Sensing and Thinking (ST)	Intuition and Feeling (NF)
Take roll	Help teacher organize things
Coach others	Tutor peers
Safety patrol	Work on school service projects
ROTC duties	Help with things that require attention to detail
Put flag up	
Assist in office	
Monitor cafeteria	
Collect papers	
Be a team captain	
Collect lunch money	
Run school store	
Operate audio-visuals	

Sensing and Feeling (SF)	Intuition and Thinking (NT)
Tutor peers	Organize others
Help others	Teach others
Office helper	Student representative on school improvement team
Safety patrol	Teacher assistant
Library assistant	

As is typical, the ST types can always think of specific action-oriented tasks and lots of them! The SF types emphasize service in a helping sense. The NT types like being a leader of others in some way, and the NF types join the SF types in emphasizing service. Become more proficient at recognizing the positive and negative expression of each of the four functions so you can decide when to praise and when to intervene with other options.

Myers gives a summary of the positive and negative expressions that can be applied to school settings.[8]

Myers goes on to say that making use of the functions in negative expressions only serves to develop them in inferior, negative ways.

Examples of Positive Expression	*Examples of Negative Expression*
Sensing: Seeing and facing facts.	**Sensing:** Indulging this function by running away from a problem to a trivial amusement.
Intuition: Seeing a possibility and making it happen.	**Intuition:** Giving in to this function by dreaming up impossibilities that would provide an effortless solution.
Thinking: Analyzing the probable consequences of a proposed action and deciding accordingly.	**Thinking:** Yielding to this function by criticizing anyone who has an opposite view of a problem.
Feeling: Considering what matters most to oneself and others.	**Feeling:** Indulging this function by rehearsing how right and blameless one has been all along.

Tips for Helping Students Work from Preferences and Practice the Opposites

For students who prefer Extraversion	For students who prefer Introversion
• Allow opportunity for students to work interactively and also encourage them to introvert by writing and reflecting briefly before answering or taking action.	• Allow these students to know it is OK to work alone on a particular assignment. Also let them know you would like them to tell another student about their project once it is completed.
• Tell students ahead of time that they will be allowed to respond aloud a maximum of two times to a particular topic. Invite them to choose their comments with this in mind. What do they *most* want to say?	• Tell the class before a class discussion ensues what the topic is and that everyone will be expected to respond. This gives Introverts a chance to reflect and get their thoughts together in order to communicate more comfortably to the rest of the class.
• With younger students, use "speak-up tickets." Each student is given two tickets to use in a given discussion. They may use their tickets at any time during the discussion but have only two tickets to spend.	• Encourage Introverted students to ask for time for internal processing when either the teacher or other students do not remember this may be needed.

For students who prefer Sensing	For students who prefer Intuition
• Invite students to restate the lesson objective or the goal of a project in language that is clearer or more concise. • Encourage students with a Sensing preference to assist with planning of the ultimate direction a project will take. • Help students see the overall purpose of an activity or project. • Help students brainstorm possibilities regarding a potential project or options for carrying it out. • Teach the skill of mind mapping to develop new ideas and options (see Resource 16, *Mind Mapping and Mind Structuring*, for details).	Help students with a preference for Intuition to work out step-by-step plans for accomplishing an assignment or project. Help them notice any important detail they have overlooked. Remind them to include supporting evidence for their conclusions when appropriate. Encourage them to make use of existing knowledge and resources as well as new ideas when carrying out an assignment or project. When their minds wander, suggest they make a note with key words of their tangential thoughts to revisit at a later time. (Sticky notes are good for this.) Teach the skill of mind structuring to help students learn to pay attention to relevant factual information (see Resource 16, *Mind Mapping and Mind Structuring*).

For students who prefer Thinking	For students who prefer Feeling
• Encourage students with a preference for Thinking to allow themselves and others to make mistakes as they experiment and take risks. • Encourage them to ask, "Who?" as well as "What?" or "Why?" when working on assignments. • Encourage them to praise classmates while a project is underway and to celebrate each others' small victories—not just the big one at the end.	• Encourage students with a preference for Feeling to take criticism as information only. ("Receive and review before you accept or reject" is how our colleague Larry Collins phrases it.) • Encourage them to ask "Why?" as well as "Who?" • Encourage them to be willing to agree to disagree. • Encourage them to express feedback to others or state their opinions directly.

With Thinking–Feeling differences it is often helpful to initiate actions when students have engaged their preferred function but could benefit from use of the opposite. Morale and motivation can plummet without sensitivity here. For example, when you overhear a blunt comment from a Thinking type to a Feeling type and see hurt reflected in the latter's face, you can validate both preferences as well as provide a model that acknowledges and engages both functions.

Example:

Thinking-type Ben to Feeling-type Julie:

"Julie, what you did caused the whole project to slow down!"

Teacher to Julie (and as a model to Ben):

"Julie, you really believed what you did would work so it was worth a try. Ben stated his perspective honestly. I hope you can take what he said and decide for yourself whether you agree or not."

Teacher to Ben:

"Not all thoughts have to be stated. However, if you believe a statement needs to be voiced, then try finding a way to do so without hurting someone's feelings. It helps to change a "you did something" statement to "I felt . . . when you" statement. One option might be to say, "I was really frustrated when the project slowed down after your (action)."

RESOURCES

RESOURCE 15, *Helping Students Develop Their Preferences: Teacher Tips,* suggests additional ideas for helping students develop use of all preferences.

Tips for Teachers to Engage Opposite Functions

Extraversion and Introversion

- When asking questions of two or more students in a group, pause at least five seconds before allowing anyone to answer. This approach gives the Introverts a chance to process internally what you have asked and form a response, and it gives the Extraverts a chance to develop their Introversion—even if for only a few seconds!

- Intermingle Extraverted and Introverted students when forming groups and remind them to accommodate and practice both directions of energy.

Sensing and Intuition

1. *Ask students to do the following:*
   - In one sentence, summarize themes represented in the material being studied.
   - Provide at least five facts that support these themes.

Ask students to discuss if either task was more difficult for them. Point out that one is easier than the other for most of us and that this is normal. Also point out the importance of both overall themes and supporting data.

2. *Pair students with a preference for Sensing with students who have a preference for Intuition. Give them the following directions:*
   a. Ask the Sensing student to tell the Intuitive student about his or her work. Ask the student preferring Intuition to learn as many details as possible, asking for more if necessary.
   b. Ask the student preferring Intuition to give the Sensing student just three important pieces of information regarding his or her work. The Sensing student is then to guess the gist of the work and report a summary of his or her understanding to the Intuitive student.

Process this exercise with the students in terms of ease and difficulty. Emphasize the importance of both overall understanding and supporting details.

Thinking and Feeling

1. *Pair Thinking students with Feeling students. Based on a piece of work they have each completed individually:*
   a. Ask students with a preference for Thinking to explain the potential impact of their ideas on people's lives.
   b. Ask the students with a preference for Feeling to state one to three logical conclusions that can be drawn from their work.

2. *Ask students to discuss what the experience of using their less preferred function is like. Discuss the importance to communication of being able to do so (e.g., when trying to get someone of a different type to accept your idea).*

Judging and Perceiving

1. *Give students a passage to read or have them listen to a recording or watch a video and then do the following:*
   a. Ask the students with a preference for Judging to formulate at least three open-ended questions about the material.
   b. Ask the students with a preference for Perceiving to make at least three declarative statements about the material.

2. *Discuss what the experience is like for each of the groups, relating their responses to differences between Judging and Perceiving.*

Personalizing pathways to achievement, while presenting a teacher with new challenges, offers the rewards of increased motivation, higher achievement, greater self-concept, and fewer discipline problems. It's not a bad investment!

In a Nutshell

- Type is not static. It is developed over time.
- Good type development means individuals first develop their natural pre-dispositions for perception (Sensing or Intuition) and judgment (Thinking or Feeling) with their opposite functions used in a supportive role.
- Ideally, by the time a young person reaches adulthood, the first two functions are well-developed so there is a solid way of forming perceptions and making judgments.
- In adulthood the third and fourth functions emerge more in the personality over time and claim more expression in a person's life as the individual matures.
- Self-awareness of natural and less-preferred mental functions can help students become more skilled in the kinds of intelligences that may not be natural to them individually.
- Classrooms are fertile environments for developing type when teachers incorporate type appropriately into the educational structure.

Check Your Understanding

Q *Is there a hierarchy of type development for each of the types? If so, describe it.*

A Yes. All four functions do not develop into conscious use at once, nor are they developed to the same level of conscious use. Ideally, one function is dominant and develops first. While the other functions are used to some extent all along, typically they develop over time. Usually the auxiliary function develops next. In our adult years the third function (the tertiary function), and the fourth function (the inferior or least-preferred function), develop more fully into conscious use. However, they generally do not develop to the same level as the first two functions.

Q *Does an Introverted type use the dominant function (S, N, F, T) in the inner or outer world?*

A Since Introverts primarily gain energy from the inner world they use their dominant function in the inner world most often.

Q *Does an Extraverted type use the dominant function (S, N, F, T) in the inner or outer world most often?*

A Since Extraverts primarily gain energy from the outer world, they use their dominant function in the outer world.

Q *Describe the relationship between the dominant and auxiliary functions and at least one benefit of this relationship.*

A The dominant function leads the personality and the auxiliary offers strong support. One function deals with perception and the other deals with judgment. One function is more often extraverted and the other is more often introverted. Successful use of the relationship between the dominant and the auxiliary fosters more effective decisions and behavior.

Q *Give some examples of ways teachers can promote type development in the classroom.*

A Teachers can do the following:

- Give students a chance to describe how they learn best and use this information to teach specific students, especially if they begin to "fall between the cracks."
- Let students know that minds learn differently and that the different ways minds are engaged are equally valuable.
- Ask students to determine their goals for themselves and to describe what they need to accomplish them.
- Offer students choices for learning activities based on type groupings.
- Encourage students to "experiment" with different groupings so they can learn to engage all the preferences.

Q *What is an advantage of teachers pausing at least five seconds before allowing students to answer questions?*

A The strategy allows Introverts time to internally process the question and formulate a response and gives Extraverts a process for developing their Introversion.

Select one of your students who seems to be struggling in your classroom or in school. Use the following guidelines to engage that student.

Early Elementary School

Focus on reading practices and achievements of the student. Ask that student to read something aloud that includes new words, and notice how the student handles these words. Check out how the student typically learns to read new words. If there is no indication of the use of phonics, then teach the student how to sound out new words phonetically and notice the response. If the student is a Sensing child, learning the sounds of the word symbols could open up a new world. If the child is an Intuitive child, it may become evident if the child seems to grasp the meaning from the encircling text and concepts.

Middle or High School

With or without the labels of type, talk to the student about the four preferences and individual learning styles. Work together to find something of interest that is to be learned in your classroom and discuss options for learning the material that are in line with how the student believes he or she learns best. Use Resource 2, *Learning Preferences by Type: Words and Activities that Work,* as a guide to discussion and ask which "function pair" seems to fit best. Together, look through word and learning activity lists or curriculum samples to come up with options that fit your particular setting. Involve the student's parents if possible. Several important criteria for achievement are being introduced at once with this activity: personalized attention, personalized learning, and parental involvement.

If the student knows type, talk specifically about the four functions and explore whether that student's preferences have been reinforced in school experiences.

If the student does not know type, see if you can hypothesize about what might be the student's dominant and auxiliary functions. Then, through conversation, think about whether the student has had this reinforced in school experiences.

6

Collaboration in Teams

School Leadership is a team sport.

MICHAEL FULLAN
The Moral Imperative of School Leadership

As the designated leader of the school, a principal is typically viewed as the responsible party for setting direction, determining goals and priorities, overseeing the instructional program, and ensuring the completion of a variety of responsibilities too numerous to name. Successful learning for each student is, of course, the primary mission of school. Because of the enormous challenges facing educators in today's schools, people must come together and work collaboratively to examine and resolve the many critical issues and problems presented by greater diversity, accountability, population growth, and public concerns. When the adults in the school work together collaboratively, students benefit.

Gerald Tirozzi, executive director of the National Association of Secondary School Principals, in the seminal work *Breaking Ranks II: Strategies for Leading High School Reform*, states that "School leaders must ask, 'Have we done enough to reach and engage each student who enters our school system, regardless of socio-economic status, ability level, or ethnic background?'"[1] This valuable resource presents thirty-one recommendations for improving high schools. The recommendations, which can also be expanded to all school levels, relate to three core areas: collaborative leadership, personalization, and curriculum.

In the current climate of education accountability and federal legislation, leaders from different schools, school board personnel, parents, community leaders, and legislators are increasingly brought together to work in collaborative teams. Many teams function superbly—generating the kind of synergy that produces creative and effective results and team members come away believing it was time well spent. Other teams often seem like a waste of time and at best produce a report that gathers dust on somebody's shelf. Our challenge is to demonstrate how the intentional use of personality type differences can lead to greater team effectiveness.

Typical teams in schools that could benefit from the applications of psychological type might include the following:

- School-improvement teams responsible for determining the overall plan for improving the school.
- Administrative teams that provide leadership and administration.
- Teams of teachers who teach the same subject or same group of students.
- Grade-level teams that focus on the curriculum and needs of students at a particular grade level.
- Departmental teams that discuss the issues related to specific academic areas.
- Leadership teams that handle important school decisions.
- School committees that deal with a variety of tasks such as cultural arts, hospitality, newsletter, and fundraising.
- Parent support-groups such as parent-teacher associations, athletic boosters, and music boosters.

Usually all parties come together assuming a cooperative partnership will develop where all perspectives will be respectfully heard and considered. However, collaborative discussions and decision-making often dissipate in the rigor of debate over different philosophies and courses of action. Whereas it may have seemed like a good idea to bring different viewpoints and skills to the table, frustration often outweighs foreseeable benefit. Sadly, the students lose when the adults cannot work together effectively.

Bringing Psychological Type to the Table

What type adds to the functioning of these collaborative teams is significant when team members have knowledge of and value the use of personality type. The benefits are many and include the following:

- When team members know type they gain an appreciation for different perspectives and have a common language that explains and clarifies differences rather than personalizes them.
- Individual team members affirm their strengths and recognize potential blind spots.
- Teams as a whole recognize their collective strengths and potential blind spots.
- Teams gain insight into situations in which conflicting perspectives may be a factor of type differences and work together to value and make use of these differences.

- Tasks and responsibilities can be delegated based on the preferences of the team members.
- Tasks and responsibilities also can be requested based on team members' desire to learn new skills and develop their less-preferred functions.
- Team members with strengths in certain areas can mentor those who want to develop in those less-skilled areas.

Ideally, the use of personality type is introduced into the agenda when the team first forms or perhaps before an existing team takes on a new task. Much team conflict and wasted time and energy can be avoided if type-based needs and requests are acknowledged early in the team effort and norms are established to accommodate the differences. When conflict occurs, extricating the type differences that have encroached on the process allows a team to focus on the issues that brought them together.

Determining Team Strengths and Potential Difficulties

There are two activities that many teams have found helpful in undertaking to recognize strengths and difficulties. The first exercise helps team members evaluate, understand, and discuss the team's psychological makeup. The second exercise is especially suited for teams with more limited knowledge of psychological type.

Exercise 1: Team Evaluation

1. Develop a type table indicating each member's type.
2. Discuss what each preference can uniquely contribute to problem solving and to the team's process.
3. Determine the number of members who represent each of the eight preferences (e.g., how many prefer Extraversion and how many prefer Introversion?).
4. Note which preferences are particularly well represented and likely represent team strengths.
5. Note which preferences are absent or under-represented, and discuss the implications for intentional inclusion of these contributions.

NOTE: These team-analysis resources can still be used when some or all team members do not have type knowledge. By showing team members, for example, that *process* (N) as well as *content* (S) is important and by offering opportunity for *reflection* (I) and *discussion* (E), the team leader can impart the nuances of type even for those less familiar with it.

Exercise 2: Increasing Team Effectiveness

- Give team members copies of Resource 22, *Type Specific Tips for Problem Solving*, and ask them individually to read the tips for their preferences and decide if they agree or disagree.

RESOURCES

RESOURCE 18, *Team Analysis*, provides suggestions for personal reflection and team discussion. RESOURCE 19, *Type Tables*, includes a blank type table for recording the team diagnosis. The type table is a useful tool for visualizing and analyzing the strengths and potential blind spots of a team.

- Ask members to point out to each other which tips they would appreciate their team members practicing as they work together.
- In summary, remind team members of the contributions each of the preferences makes and tell them that the team members need each other to be a more effective team. Accommodating differences requires learning new behaviors and, therefore, it is helpful to remind members that patience also is required when practicing new skills.

Remember the importance of *confidentiality* in using type! While people are free to share information about themselves, team members and others who know an individual's type preferences, should keep that information confidential unless the individual gives permission for it to be shared with others outside the team. Trust is the basic ingredient for any team to work at its highest performance level.

Case Studies for Team Work

The following case studies provide a vehicle for team members to analyze the composition of teams and discuss how to use their knowledge of personality type differences to increase their effectiveness as a collaborative team.

CASE STUDY 1:
Using Type Differences to Increase Collaborative Team Effectiveness

A subcommittee of the school improvement team was chosen to examine the problem of tardy students and make recommendations for changes to current policies and procedures. The team consisted of an INTJ, an ENFJ, an ESTJ, an INFP, and an ENTJ. The team completed Resource 18, *Team Analysis*. The team leader then facilitated a discussion about their team. (A team leader may be selected in advance or determined by the committee.)

110

Figure 6.1 *Type Table for Team Analysis—Case Study*

ISTJ	ISFJ	INFJ	INTJ
			X
ISTP	ISFP	INFP	INTP
		X	
ESTP	ESFP	ENFP	ENTP
ESTJ	ESFJ	ENFJ	ENTJ
X		**X**	**X**

Extraverts 3	Introverts 2
Sensing 1	Intuition 4
Thinking 3	Feeling 2
Judging 4	Perceiving 1
ST 1	SF 0
NF 2	NT 2

The team identified the following strengths of their team:

- There is a good balance between Introverts and Extraverts and Thinking types and Feeling types.
- The ENFJ will be particularly sensitive to the needs and feelings of the team members and will strive to assist the members in working together cooperatively.
- The INFP and the ENFJ will likely ensure important human values will be taken into consideration in developing a plan or program to solve the tardy problem.

- The ESTJ will work to see that the team stays task-focused, that data is analyzed, and that the recommended solution to the problem is practical, realistic, and followed through to implementation.
- The INTJ and ENTJ will provide leadership related to the examination of larger issues and goals with a focus on change and improvement to current policy.
- The high percentage of members with a preference for Intuition (INTJ, ENTJ, ENFJ, and INFP) means the group is likely to be creative and innovative and will bring multiple options to the table as they work to develop an effective policy.
- The Judging types will see that the group works steadily and stays aware of any set deadline.

The team identified the following potential weaknesses of their team:
- Since there is only one Sensing type on the team, the team may not pay enough attention to the reality of the problem and may not collect the specific data and information needed to get a firm understanding of the problem and come up with a realistic, workable solution.
- There is only one Perceiving type (INFP) on the team. The other members may be inclined to cut off discussion before they have considered all the possible ways to solve the problem.
- There may be friction between the INTJ, the ENTJ, and the ESTJ over issues of leadership.
- The ENTJ, INTJ, and ESTJ may become impatient with the ENFJ and INFP who believe it is important to have some flexibility that takes into consideration the individual situations of the students who have valid reasons for being tardy. The Thinking types will tend to believe that if the policy is to be fair, any student who is tardy should receive the same consequences without consideration of the reasons for the tardiness.
- The ENFJ enjoys people and wants the team members to work together in a harmonious, friendly relationship and may seem too unfocused for the INTJ, ENTJ, and ESTJ and perhaps to the INFP.
- The ENTJ, INTJ, and ESTJ may prefer to look at the tardy situation logically and objectively without taking special situations into consideration.
- The ENFJ and INFP may become frustrated when the INTJ, ENTJ, and ESTJ want to conduct a logical analysis of the problem without including a discussion of any of the personal reasons why students are tardy.
- The ESTJ may resist implementing an innovative idea that hasn't already been implemented in other schools, preferring instead to stick to the tried-and-true programs.
- The INTJ and INFP may feel frustrated when the Extraverts on the team take a lot of "air time."

The team members agreed to the following ways they could work together to increase their effectiveness:

- Gather sufficient data to examine the current situation before beginning any discussion of possible solutions.

- Consider the practical implications of their recommendations.

- Listen to each other and consider all of the opinions and ideas of the members without cutting off the discussion in the interest of closure.

- Strive to work together in a positive manner and to respect differences of opinion as helpful.

- Be open to additional ideas, even if some of the members feel they have discussed the problem long enough and want to decide on a recommended solution.

- Recognizing the Introverts' need to think through the ideas internally before sharing their opinions, the Extraverts agreed to give the Introverts time to think about the ideas rather than expecting an immediate response.

- Recognizing the need for Extraverts to brainstorm ideas and solutions before they determine their best ideas and solutions, the Introverts agreed to listen to the entire process rather than immediately evaluate the ideas the Extraverts suggested.

> **TIP**
>
> *For a more in-depth analysis of this team note the various dominant functions of each team member, which may indicate where each person is more likely to either (a) enter the decision-making process or (b) desire to get to a solution as quickly as possible. When members are focusing on very different concerns, miscommunication or poor listening is often the result. (See chapter 5 for discussion of the dominant function.)*

A strong leader welcomes the presence of differences. The following case study illustrates how one principal used knowledge of type to increase the effectiveness of an administrative team.

CASE STUDY 2:
Using Type to Create a Successful Administrative Team

Background Information

This case study is based on an actual administrative team of a large urban high school and illustrates how one principal worked with the members of the administrative team to determine job responsibilities using type preferences and interests of the individuals. The assignment of responsibilities was frequently made based on team members' strengths and interests, but in some instances responsibilities were assigned to allow the administrators to develop greater skill in certain areas including the development of their less-preferred functions.

The Administrative Team

The five-person administrative team consisted of Sue, the principal (INTJ), and four assistant principals: James (ESTJ), Lynn (ESFJ), Laura (INFJ), and Robert (ESTP). The principal felt fortunate to be able to work with a group of administrators who brought different strengths and areas of interest so there would be strength in diversity. Figure 6.2 shows a type table with the preferences of each team member.

Figure 6.2 *Type Table of an Administrative Team—Case Study*

ISTJ	ISFJ	INFJ	INTJ
		Laura *Assistant Principal*	Sue *Principal*
ISTP	ISFP	INFP	INTP
ESTP	ESFP	ENFP	ENTP
Robert *Assistant Principal*			
ESTJ	ESFJ	ENFJ	ENTJ
James *Assistant Principal*	Lynn *Assistant Principal*		

Sue, principal. With preferences for INTJ, Sue views herself as a strategic planner with a clear vision about the direction for the school. Her strengths are in design, analysis, organization, and problem solving. She constantly searches for ways to improve procedures, administrative practices, programs, student activities, and curriculum. She is driven by her vision.

Her enthusiasm and energy have a motivating effect on many of the people in the school; however, she sometimes overlooks the importance of taking time to build relationships and does not always pay enough attention to the human factor in the decision-making process.

She is very interested in developing the natural talents of her administrative team and the other people in the school. Through both modeling and teaching, she helps others develop new areas of expertise. She also tries to learn from others.

James, assistant principal. As an ESTJ, James views himself as a loyal and dedicated member of the administrative team. He enjoys performing tasks quickly and efficiently and can be counted on to gather all the relevant facts before making a decision. He is an expert on many aspects of school operations including heating and air conditioning, electrical systems, and plumbing. He was an industrial arts teacher before entering school administration and is able to fix almost anything!

James has a logical mind and focuses on results. He is clear and direct when dealing with students, teachers, and parents. Organization is his strength, and he always follows through on assignments. His responsibilities as an assistant principal include transportation, parking, textbooks, teacher evaluation, and student discipline.

Lynn, assistant principal. With preferences for ESFJ, Lynn is the peacemaker on the administrative team. She is a good listener and people naturally turn to her for guidance and support. She wants to maintain harmonious relationships and is very considerate of people's feelings. She does not like conflict and will do whatever she can to resolve it, even if it means additional work for her.

She completes all assigned tasks accurately and on time. She enjoys assignments that require close attention to detail. If she checks a memo, policy, or announcement, for example, and says it is correct, you know it is! Her responsibilities as an assistant principal include the master schedule, maintaining the school calendar, student activities, teacher evaluation, and student discipline.

Laura, assistant principal. Laura (INFJ) is a creative innovator who focuses on key issues in education such as the quality of the instructional program, ways to meet the needs of students at risk, and professional development activities for teachers. Because of her interest in global issues and her ideas and insight, she helps others see the big picture and focus on possibilities. As an Introvert, she does not always openly share her personal thoughts but will when encouraged to do so. She has a quiet manner and firm convictions.

Laura's sense of humor is not immediately noticed, but laughter is an important part of her life, which is evident as you get to know her. Her responsibilities as an assistant principal include curriculum and instruction, staff development, coordinating a mentor program for first-year teachers, teacher evaluation, and student discipline.

Robert, assistant principal. Robert (ESTP) is a creative problem solver who enjoys finding ways to take care of any situation no matter how difficult or seemingly impossible. He tends to make decisions quickly, frequently collecting data through use of his senses. He enjoys people and spends a good part of his time talking to students, teachers, and parents. He is energetic, has a positive outlook, and brings a fresh and original approach to solving routine problems.

His cleverness sometimes gets him in difficulty, but he has such an endearing manner that people usually forgive him even if he doesn't follow the rules. His responsibilities include maintenance of the building, supervision of the custodial staff, campus beautification, teacher evaluation, and student discipline.

Analysis of the Team

The administrative team is well-balanced in terms of Extraverts and Introverts, and those with preferences for Sensing and Intuition, and Thinking and Feeling. There is only one person (Robert, ESTP) who has a preference for Perceiving, and he brings spontaneity to the team. When most team members may prefer bringing closure to a situation, Robert helps the team consider other options. Robert's enjoyment of trouble shooting and his natural tendency to "take care of things," even if it means ignoring the rules or school district policies, sometimes frustrates other members of the team, especially James (ESTJ) who believes in always following established policies and procedures.

The combination of members with preferences for Sensing and Intuition enables the team to consider future possibilities and innovations as well as the practical, realistic aspects of implementation. Members with preferences for Thinking and Judging (Sue, the INTJ principal, and James, ESTJ assistant principal) are naturally in tune with each other. They use objective analysis and logic to solve problems and are frequently called on to make the difficult decisions, ones they do not shy away from making.

Laura, the INFJ assistant principal brings a quiet strength to the team. Lynn, the ESFJ assistant principal is a consensus builder who encourages cooperation among members of the administrative team, faculty, students, and staff. Others sometimes take advantage of her good nature and interest in building harmonious relationships. She doesn't really like to handle controversial issues although she will when necessary. The team is missing ENF types who would likely be the natural, enthusiastic innovators on the team.

"You tell me of degrees of perfection to which human nature is capable of arriving, and I believe it, but at the same time lament that our admiration should arise from the scarcity of the instances."

ABIGAIL ADAMS (1744–1818) Wife of the second president and mother of the sixth, Abigail Adams is known for her politically and socially insightful correspondence with her husband, John Adams, who was often away from home forging a new nation while she raised children and managed their Massachusetts farm.

The principal who has knowledge of type preferences is willing to allow individuals to determine job responsibilities based on interests and strengths. She finds that this approach increases the effectiveness of the school organization as well as the job satisfaction of the people involved!

Determining Job Responsibilities

In deciding on specific administrative responsibilities, the team members discussed the various assignments, along with the strengths and interests of individual team members. They realized that although self-selection was a top priority for determining responsibilities, someone would have to agree to take each responsibility. Because of the diversity of the team, this task was not difficult. Working together, the administrative team members decided on the job responsibilities each person would assume. In addition, team members indicated a desire to develop their least-preferred functions. They agreed to seek help from each other in order to accomplish this.

Professional Development: Developing the Least-Preferred Function

James (ESTJ) recognized his strengths in organization, but wanted to develop his least-preferred function, Intuition. By volunteering to coordinate the planning process for implementing a peer-mediation program at the school, he was able to work on an innovative project that required him to use his intuition. By exchanging ideas with the other Intuitives on the team he was able to successfully design a new and innovative program for the school.

Lynn (ESFJ) is meticulous about completing assignments with accuracy and precision. She knew this area of expertise would be helpful in the process of building a master schedule. Placing students in the correct classes requires attention to detail. As changes were made in the master schedule, Lynn checked carefully at each step in the process to prevent errors.

Building a master schedule also requires problem-solving skills, including the ability to see relationships among the different aspects of the schedule and figuring out ways to resolve conflicting demands. These big-picture skills come

CHAPTER 6
Collaboration
in Teams

naturally to Intuitives. Lynn learned these skills through coaching and observing Sue, the INTJ principal, as she worked on the schedule. Sue made a conscious effort to verbalize her thought processes as she considered the various possibilities for scheduling classes in the master schedule. Consequently, Lynn was able to learn how a person with a preference for Intuition looks at possibilities and selects a solution.

Laura, (INFJ) had an aura of mystery about her, and she was not well known among the faculty. She was extremely responsible and genuinely interested in helping others grow professionally. She did excellent work but many people were unaware of it. Sue, the principal, encouraged her to share what she had accomplished and be more "public" about her work and successes. Sue also publicly recognized Laura periodically to make others aware of her work.

Robert (ESTP) brought spontaneity to the team. He was quick to see problems and rushed to handle them. He sometimes bypassed established policies and procedures as he was so intent on taking care of a situation as quickly as possible. His disregard for tradition and established procedures sometimes created tension on the team, especially with James, the ESTJ assistant principal. Sue, the principal, helped Robert by recognizing his creative problem-solving ability while at the same time helping him see the necessity of complying with policies and procedures (except, perhaps, on rare occasions where justification could be made for not following the rules).

As this case study illustrates, a principal who knows type can facilitate a successful team where members' strengths and interests are utilized. A principal who knows type can also encourage others to develop new skills and increase their knowledge by learning from others and continuing to develop least-preferred preferences.

To Wrap It Up

Working in collaborative teams, while presenting new challenges for principals and teachers, offers the rewards of higher morale and greater motivation; increases in administrative support, creative ideas, and best practices; and higher student achievement. It's not a bad investment!

In a Nutshell

- Personality type provides a useful tool to help collaborative teams enhance team work and make constructive use of differences.
- Use of type significantly increases the effectiveness of collaborative teams and brings many benefits.

- Teams can determine their strengths and potential difficulties through a team diagnosis for improving team effectiveness.
- Type can be used to create a successful administrative team and determine job responsibilities using team members' strengths and the individual interests of the team members.
- With type knowledge, potential blind spots of a team can be anticipated and addressed.
- Team members who know type have a common language that explains and clarifies differences and teaches people to appreciate different perspectives.
- Teams gain insight into how conflicting perspectives may be a factor of type differences and how such differences can be an asset to the team.

Check Your Understanding

Scenario: An administrative team of five people completed a team analysis of type as shown in figure 6.3.

Figure 6.3 *Type Table of an Administrative Team*

ISTJ **1**	ISFJ	INFJ	INTJ
ISTP	ISFP	INFP	INTP
ESTP	ESFP	ENFP	ENTP **1**
ESTJ **1**	ESFJ	ENFJ	ENTJ **2**

Q *What are some strengths of the team?*

A The team is strong on analysis and problem solving. Team members express their ideas freely and openly. The team has a good balance between Sensing and Intuition. The team will consider the practical implications and look at possibilities realistically. The team has members who prefer details and structure and those who can see the big picture and possible implications. The team is creative and futuristic and can come up with a variety of possibilities. There are four team members who prefer Judging, and so the team is likely to be organized and complete tasks and responsibilities in a timely manner.

Q *What are some potential blind spots, and how can the team try to avoid problems based on the types represented on the team?*

A Since no one on the team has a preference for Feeling, the team may tend to make decisions objectively using logical analysis without considering the feelings of those affected by the decisions. Team members may need to make an intentional effort to consider the impact of decisions on people and take into account the importance of harmony in relationships. There may be a clash for who's in charge with three team members (the two ENTJs and one ESTJ) having natural preferences for ETJ.

There is only one team member who prefers Perceiving. This person may become frustrated if the other team members move to closure too soon. This team member can help by encouraging members to stay flexible and keep their options open as long as possible.

Getting Started

- Use Resource 18, *Team Analysis*, for a school team you belong to. Discuss with the other team members the strengths and potential blind spots of the team that can be anticipated from the types represented.

- When a team you belong to is asked to complete a project, discuss ways your team can make constructive use of type differences. Discuss ideas for completing the project and then delegate specific tasks based on team members' preferences.

7

Collaboration in Decision Making and Problem Solving

Coming together, sharing together, working together, and succeeding together.

AUTHOR UNKNOWN

In our work in schools, we know that principals, teachers, and students are often criticized for the decisions they make. Principals are often asked to over-turn a teacher's decision, for example, and students and parents frequently seek out counselors or administrators when they don't agree with a teacher's decision. A parent who is unhappy with a decision by the principal may say she will go to the school board or the school superintendent if the principal doesn't change the decision. All these possibilities for misunderstandings and differences make the use of psychological type an important tool in creating harmony and efficiency among school-related teams, whose ultimate goal is to provide the best education possible for the students.

People with different type preferences typically approach the process of decision making and problem solving in different ways, and may sometimes even achieve the same result. Although you may not agree with a person's process or decision, you can better understand it if you acknowledge and recognize the impact of type differences.

An exercise that teams may find helpful involves the intentional use of type in problem solving and decision making. Isabel Myers stressed the importance of including all four mental functions sequentially in decision making and pointed out that the tendency for people is to emphasize their two preferences while overlooking the other two. When people overlook blind spots, they omit impor-tant steps necessary for a more complete and accurate perception and a wiser judgment.

The Z decision-making and problem-solving model developed by Gordon Lawrence[1] illustrates how to use all four functions in the sequence suggested by Myers. Ideally, each of the steps in the Z-model addresses one of the specific components of optimal problem solving and decision making:

Sensing Gather as much factual information as possible relevant to the issue or problem.

Consider where the situation has been encountered before and what has worked or not worked.

Intuition Generate as many options for solutions as possible based on this information, censoring none.

Pay attention to hunches and gut reactions.

Thinking Evaluate the pros and cons of each option generated.

Determine the logical consequences of each one.

Feeling Evaluate the impact on people of each option.

Include the input of all involved in the decision making.

Figure 7.1 *Z Decision-Making and Problem-Solving Model*

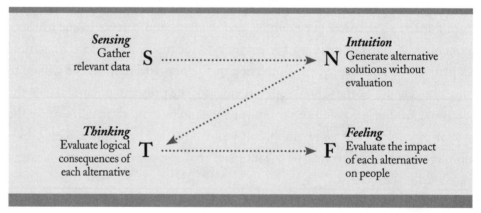

The Z-model (figure 7.1) helps you visualize the two steps you are likely to emphasize in the process (your preferences) and the two steps you need to be more *intentional* about including.

For instance, Sondra, with preferences for Intuition and Feeling, naturally puts emphasis on brainstorming alternatives and considering how each would potentially have impact on people. She may overlook some realistic data that could affect the alternatives she generates and could easily ignore the logical analysis that could tell her why her favorite solution wouldn't work.

Diane, with preferences for Intuition and Thinking, also puts emphasis on brainstorming alternatives but evaluates those alternatives for their logical consequences. Without some intentionality, she could overlook some realistic and important data, as well as how the alternatives under consideration could affect people individually.

As a decision-making team, our duo is particularly strong on generating possibilities, and working together we are likely to evaluate each possibility for both logical consequences and the impact on people. But without awareness, we may miss some important facts or details that could derail all of our prized ideas, forcing us to begin the decision making process all over again.

In a similar fashion, each of your team members can refer to the model and note their own strengths and potential blind spots based on their preferences and then the team as a whole can do the same. This awareness suggests the particular steps that need special attention. People with preferences for Sensing and Thinking will need to be intentional about using Intuition and Feeling. People with preferences for Intuition and Feeling will need to be intentional about using Sensing and Thinking. People with preferences for Sensing and Feeling will need to be intentional about using Intuition and Thinking. People with preferences for Intuition and Thinking will need to be intentional about using Sensing and Feeling.

Strategies Used for Decision Making by Type Preferences

People with different preferences will use different strategies for decision making. These strategies are as follows.

Sensing and Thinking (ST)

- Will look at the facts of the situation.
- Will analyze the situation and use logic to arrive at a decision.
- Will work efficiently to reach a resolution.
- May make a decision early and not consider additional possibilities.
- May not consider the impact on people individually.

Sensing and Feeling (SF)

- Will consider the impact of a decision on people.
- Are interested in the facts and realism, not in abstract theories.
- Usually will involve others in arriving at a decision.
- May make a decision before sufficient options have been considered.
- May not step outside the situation and look at it objectively.

Intuition and Feeling (NF)

- Are concerned about others and how the decision will affect people.
- Will involve others in the decision-making process and look at alternatives and possibilities.
- May overlook important data relevant to the situation.
- Value harmony and may have difficulty with a decision that has a negative impact on others, no matter how logical that decision is to others.

Intuition and Thinking (NT)

- Will use logical analysis and principles to make a decision.
- Will use a rational, impersonal approach to decision making.
- Concern for how people will be affected is secondary.
- May overlook important data relevant to the situation.
- Will use others to generate possible alternatives but typically like to make the decision independently.

GREAT MINDS

"In the fields of observation chance favors only those minds which are prepared."

LOUIS PASTEUR (1822–1895) This French scientist revolutionized biology and methods of public health through his discoveries of how disease-causing bacteria and viruses work, which led to the introduction of vaccines as well as sanitary medical practices and food preparation, known as "pasteurization."

Strategies Used for Problem Solving by Type Preferences

Problem solving is an ongoing challenge for school personnel, and differences in approaches to problem solving abound. Not all aspects of the different ways of solving problems relate to type, but there are some striking type differences that, if acknowledged, can greatly increase the effectiveness of the problem solving process. If ignored, the process of problem solving itself can potentially become a conflict due to type differences. It is thus helpful to be aware not only of our own preferred approach to problem solving, but also to understand how type differences affect the ways others view situations and approach problem solving. It is often helpful to disengage the type issues first before dealing with any of the other issues in a situation.

Extraversion (E)

- Want to talk about the problem.
- Will verbalize ideas, thoughts, and feelings.
- Need time to discuss the situation.
- May suggest several ways to resolve the problem.
- Are willing to discuss the advantages and disadvantages of each suggestion for solving the problem.

Introversion (I)

- Need time to reflect and think about the problem.
- May prefer to put feelings, ideas, and suggestions in writing rather than talk about them.
- May initially refuse to discuss the problem.
- May need time to think about the possible options for solving the problem before discussing any of them.

Sensing (S)

- Interested in the facts of the situation.
- Want specific, practical, and realistic solutions presented in an orderly fashion.
- May want the solution to the problem put in writing.
- Will follow-up to be certain the agreed upon plan was followed.

Intuition (N)

- Interested in the meaning of the situation.
- Will look for implications beyond the facts of the situation.
- Will become bored or irritated if given too many facts and too many specifics.
- Will look for ways to settle the immediate problem and also for ways to prevent a similar problem from developing in the future.
- Want solutions that have long-range impact.

Thinking (T)

- Want an impersonal, objective, and rational analysis of the problem.
- Will use logic to determine the appropriate way to solve the problem.
- Want a solution that is designed to get at the causes of the problem.
- Will work for an efficient resolution.

Feeling (F)

- Want to find a solution that is agreeable to everyone.
- Concerned about the needs, interests, and feelings of the people involved.
- Will use their system of personal values to try to find a harmonious solution to the problem.
- Whenever possible, want the problem solved by consensus or mutual agreement.

Judging (J)

- Will strive for order and structure.
- Will help keep a group focused towards a resolution.
- May want closure before all the information is in.
- May not be open to additional suggestions after a resolution has been reached.

Perceiving (P)

- Want to stay open to suggestions and options.
- Will usually not want to bring about a resolution too quickly.
- Are usually comfortable re-opening the process if additional information or ideas become available.

Problem-Solving Strategies of School Principals

Evidence of differences in type-related problem-solving strategies is apparent in a study conducted by Donald Lueder. Lueder analyzed the problem-solving strategies of 86 elementary school principals and found there were significant differences in the strategies of principals with different psychological types. [2]

Sensing (S) and Intuition (N)

Characteristically, principals with a preference for Sensing generally limit their perceptions to an immediate situation, utilizing the facts that are given. They tend to follow policy or guidelines if they exist and develop them if they don't.

Principals with a preference for Intuition characteristically perceive the situation in broader terms. Their concerns are often school or district wide and future oriented. They use the facts in the situation to seek possibilities, interconnections, and implications. They also typically use outside sources, research, and expert consultants.

Thinking (T) and Feeling (F)

Principals with a preference for Thinking prefer to make decisions in an impersonal, rational, and logical way. They are objective and matter-of-fact in approaching problem situations; personal warmth and concern for others is secondary to impersonal analysis. These principals value fairness and consistency, and while they sometimes involve others, they often make the decisions themselves or seek a compromise.

Principals with a preference for Feeling, on the other hand, generally place personal warmth and concern for others over the impersonal analysis of data. They involve others in the decision-making process where possible. They characteristically value harmony and relationships and are sensitive to conflict reduction through compassion and commitment. They are likely to attempt to reach consensus, or at least a compromise with the intent to reduce conflict.

> **RESOURCES**
>
> See **RESOURCE 20**, *Research Summary: Principals' Problem-Solving Strategies.*

Application of Problem-Solving Strategies

Because there seem to be clear patterns to problem solving by type, we can use this information when problems occur, approaching people in light of our knowledge of differences, and reminding ourselves of our capacity to use our less-preferred functions, attitudes, and orientations. We can ask ourselves the following questions:

Extraversion–Introversion

Have I . . .

- Given sufficient time to discuss the problem? (Extraversion)
- Given sufficient time to think about the problem? (Introversion)
- Given those who prefer writing their thoughts down rather than speaking them, a chance to do so? (Introversion)
- Encouraged everyone to share their thoughts and suggestions for solving the problem either verbally or in writing? (Extraversion and Introversion)

Sensing–Intuition

Have I…

- Gathered or given sufficient facts and details about the situation? (Sensing)

- Given enough attention to the implications and meaning of the situation? (Intuition)

- Discussed specific, practical, and realistic solutions? (Sensing)

- Discussed creative, innovative, future-oriented solutions? (Intuition)

- Presented the problem clearly and concisely without "beating around the bush?" (Sensing)

- Presented the "big picture" without being hung up on the details when describing the problem initially? (Intuition)

Thinking–Feeling

Have I…

- Given opportunity for an impersonal, objective, and rational analysis of the problem? (Thinking)

- Given opportunity for discussion of the needs, interests, and feelings of the people involved? (Feeling)

- Presented the facts and steps to the solution in a logical order? (Thinking)

- Noted areas of agreement? (Feeling)

- Given time to determine possible solutions that could be agreeable to everyone? (Feeling)

- Discussed the long-range impact of possible solutions? (Thinking)

Judging–Perceiving

Have I…

- Presented the problem in an organized manner? (Judging)

- Presented several possible solutions and allowed a choice? (Perceiving)

- Recognized and acknowledged the need for closure? (Judging)

- Recognized and acknowledged the desire for flexibility and a variety of options? (Perceiving)

- Encouraged those who want quick closure to be willing to consider additional solutions? (Judging)

- Encouraged those who want to continue to remain flexible and open to suggestions to come to closure after a certain point? (Perceiving)

Tip: Type-Specific Tips for Problem Solving

When acknowledging the problem-solving strategies preferred by each type, the following tips are worth remembering:

Extraversion

- Give Extraverts time to discuss the problem.
- Do not expect the first suggestion for solving the problem to be their final suggestion. Since Extraverts like to solve problems by talking about them, the first solution presented will probably not be their final one.
- Encourage Extraverts to reflect on the possible solutions.

Introversion

- Give Introverts time to think about the problem.
- Do not expect Introverts to give you an answer immediately. Since Introverts like to think about their reactions to possible solutions, they will need time to reflect before giving their ideas and comments. They may prefer to put their thoughts and ideas in writing initially rather than talking about them.
- Encourage them to share their thoughts and ideas.

Sensing

- Focus on the specific facts and details of the problem.
- Be concrete, practical, and realistic in making suggestions for problem resolution.
- Present a structured, organized presentation of the situation.
- Present the problem and solutions clearly and concisely. Do not "beat around the bush"—come straight to the point.

Intuition

- Focus on the implications and meaning of the situation.
- Present solutions that are creative, innovative, and future-oriented.
- Present the "big picture" when describing the problem. Do not worry about not giving all the details.

Thinking

- Allow them to analyze the problem and present a logical perspective on the situation.
- Don't personalize the situation. Present the facts, be objective, discuss the issues, and brainstorm possible solutions.
- Encourage them to express their views. Ask them, "What do you think about the situation?"

Feeling

- Acknowledge their concern for the people in the situation.
- Acknowledge their personal feelings about the problem and possible solutions. Ask them, "What are you feeling?"
- Begin by talking about areas of agreement. They want harmony.

Judging

- Present the problem in an organized manner.
- Recognize and acknowledge their need for closure.

Perceiving

- Present several possible solutions to the problem and allow them to choose.
- Recognize they like flexibility and a variety of options.

To Wrap It Up

Collaborative leadership in decision making and problem solving, while presenting new challenges for principals and teachers, offers the rewards of higher morale and greater motivation, increased administrative support, new ideas, best practices, and higher student achievement. It's not a bad investment!

In a Nutshell

- There are decision-making and problem-solving strategies preferred by each type.
- It is helpful to understand our own preferred approach to decision making and problem solving and to understand how different types approach decision making and problem solving.
- Some tips and strategies for problem solving by preference:
  - Extraverts want to talk about the problem.
  - Introverts need time to reflect and think about the problem.
  - Sensing types are interested in the facts and want specific, practical, and realistic solutions to the problem.
  - Intuitives will look for implications and the meaning of the situation.
  - Thinking types want an impersonal, objective, rational analysis of the problem.
  - Feeling types want to find a solution that is agreeable to everyone.

- Judging types want the problem solved and may want closure before all the information is in.
- Perceiving types usually will not want to bring about resolution too quickly and may want to stay open to suggestions and options.

- The Z decision-making and problem-solving model can be used to address important questions and issues using all four functions of Sensing, Intuition, Thinking, and Feeling.

Check Your Understanding

Q *What may people with a preference for Sensing and Thinking need to include more intentionally in problem solving?*

A People with preferences for Sensing and Thinking are quite likely to consider realistic data and evaluate possible solutions logically and objectively. They will need to strive to generate a number of alternative solutions (Intuition) and consider how possible decisions will affect people (Feeling).

Q *What may people with a preference for Sensing and Feeling need to include more intentionally in problem solving?*

A People with preferences for Sensing and Feeling will likely consider realistic data and the impact of possible solutions on people quite naturally. They will need more intentionally to generate a number of alternative solutions (Intuition) and objectively evaluate the pros and cons of each (Thinking).

Getting Started

- Use the Z problem-solving model to make a decision. Notice which steps required you to be more intentional about their use.
- Use Resource 22, *Type Specific Tips for Problem Solving*, to address a problem and evaluate your success.
- Use Resource 21, *Case Study for Problem Solving Using the Z Model*, in a discussion with colleagues who want to practice using the Z Model.

8

Collaboration in Conflict Management

*Conflict is a given. The way you view conflict and the
way you react to it are choices.*

ORGANIZATIONAL EFFECTIVENESS GROUP

Certainly a major aspect of problem solving is managing and mediating conflict. Conflict is a normal part of life in schools and occurs at all levels in the educational process. Students have disagreements with each other and their teachers; teachers have disagreements with each other and administrators; administrators sometimes find themselves on opposite sides of an issue; parents frequently disagree with teachers and administrators. Our responses to conflict are a result of our beliefs about the nature of conflict, the messages we received from our parents and other significant people in our lives, our personalities, and our experiences with conflict.

Some people believe that conflict is negative, stressful, and damaging to relationships. Others view conflict as a positive force that can provide opportunities to find productive ways of solving problems. The following messages reflect the view of the problem solver who sees the potential for resolution when conflict is faced directly:

- If you have a problem with someone, talk to the person about it;
- Conflict is an opportunity to look for mutually satisfying solutions; or
- Conflict allows us to examine differences and ultimately to make progress.

Conflict Resolution Styles

Although there are many ways of responding to conflict, most can be categorized into five groups according to the model developed by Ralph Kilmann and Kenneth Thomas.[1] According to their observations, in conflict situations, people put different levels of energy into satisfying their own interests or in satisfying

Figure 8.1 *Conflict Resolution Styles*

the interest of the other party. If satisfying their own interests is primary, they act assertively; if accommodating the other party's interest is primary, they act cooperatively. Depending on the degree of concern with the two dimensions (assertiveness and cooperativeness), a person will respond with one of five styles. These five styles are shown in figure 8.1. According to the model, all of the styles are appropriate for certain circumstances but may not be the best choice for others.

1. Avoiding One way to deal with conflict is to avoid it. Our upbringing and experiences may have convinced us that we should avoid conflict at all costs. Messages such as the following may be imbedded in our philosophy of life: "Turn the other cheek," "Even if you aren't at fault, apologize rather than lose a friend," or "If you can't say something nice about someone, don't say anything." We will sometimes choose avoidance as a way of dealing with a problem when the issue isn't important to us or when we are "choosing our battles," and avoidance offers a chance for everybody to cool off. We may also deny the conflict exists rather than deal with it as illustrated in the following examples:

- A student whose best friend was selected for the soccer team is disappointed because he was not selected. He avoids acknowledging his feelings of hurt and disappointment by saying he did not have time for practices and didn't really want to be a part of the soccer team anyway.

- A teacher who loaned another member of her department a teaching unit she had developed finds out the teacher has told other members of the faculty that the unit contains factual and grammatical errors. Rather than discuss what she has heard, the teacher decides to avoid the other teacher and never let her borrow any of her original teaching materials again.

- An administrator who learns that a teacher called in sick but actually went out of town for a long weekend chooses not to talk to the teacher, because the teacher is a popular faculty member and the principal does not want to risk alienating the teacher.

Avoidance as a method of dealing with conflict sometimes can have consequences that we may not anticipate. Although we deny the conflict exists, we are likely to feel hurt, disappointed, or angry and show these behaviors indirectly. Failure to deal with a conflict may lead to feelings of resentment that when left unacknowledged may create difficulty in our relationships. This type of response to conflict can be categorized as "you win/I lose." "You win" because I chose not to deal with the conflict, and "I lose" because I have not expressed my feelings or tried to resolve our differences.

2. Competing (also referred to as confrontation) Conflict can be viewed as a struggle for power and an opportunity for competing. People who have received messages such as "Winning is everything," "Only the fittest survive," or "Do unto others before they do unto you," may take an aggressive approach to resolving conflicts. They may take the view of "victory at any cost" without regard to the negative impact on themselves or others.

Competing and avoiding are very different approaches to conflict. While the person who chooses avoidance will avoid dealing with conflict, the person who chooses competing will seek opportunities to confront the issue directly.

- A student who is angry that his girlfriend sat with another boy in the cafeteria at lunch, for example, may confront the boy and express his anger by hurling insults or by fighting.

Confrontations sometimes occur in situations where one individual tries to use power or authority over others to resolve the conflict. In these situations, the individual will often use tactics such as threats or appeals to authority.

- A teacher, for example, may tell a student she will report him to the principal if he doesn't abide by her request to stop talking and pay attention. The teacher, who has authority over the student, threatens the student with a higher authority and thus uses power to win the argument.

- Parents will sometimes tell a child he or she must do something "because I told you so." In these situations parents are using their power over their child as a means of settling a conflict.

- A parent whose child has been suspended may tell a principal she will report him to the superintendent and demand that a decision be overturned if the principal doesn't reverse his decision to suspend her child.

Confrontations are typically situations where there are winners and losers —"I win/you lose." People who choose the competing style want to become winners at the expense of someone else. They believe that winning is the most important thing no matter what the cost. In this competition there must also be losers.

3. Accommodating Rather than discussing the conflict, the person who chooses the accommodating style believes that "giving in" or being accommodating is more important in some situations than trying to solve the problem. Accommodators will "give in" for the sake of the relationship and may choose to apologize, or else say they agree when they really disagree but don't want to offend others.

- Amy wants to ride on the float at homecoming and so does her friend Mary, but there is only room for one of them. Rather than risk losing her friendship with Mary, Amy tells her that she doesn't want to ride on the float and is happy for Mary to have the opportunity. In this situation Mary wins and Amy loses.

- A teacher may tell a parent she's sorry for not having done more to help a child when in fact she feels she has done more than any parent could reasonably expect. Because the teacher does not wish to alienate the parent, she takes the blame for a situation even though she really doesn't feel she is responsible.

- A principal may tell a district supervisor that he agrees that the supervisor made the right choice when she asked another principal to represent the school system at an international conference even though the principal believes he should have been asked.

Certainly there are times when the best response to a conflict is accommodation: to agree, apologize, or smooth over an unfortunate situation. However, recurring conflicts that are not dealt with may have more far-reaching consequences for the individuals involved.

4. Collaborating Using collaboration to resolve conflicts is based on the premise that each person in the conflict can become a winner. This approach can be categorized as "I win/you win." By working together to find a mutually satisfying resolution to the conflict, both parties become winners. Collaboration involves the parties working together to arrive at a solution that will enable both of them to meet their interests. They try to find a win-win solution so there will be no losers. By exploring each others' needs and interests, the parties find a mutually satisfying resolution to their conflict.

- A principal received a donation of several thousand dollars designated for technology. Several teams wanted the funds to be used for an expert to conduct technology training for teachers and others wanted the funds to purchase additional computers in individual classrooms. There wasn't enough money to do what each group wanted.

  The principal brought the team leaders together to resolve their differences. The parties identified their underlying issues as increased accessibility to computers versus the desire for the latest technology training. They were able to accommodate both needs when the group determined they could use some of the funds for outside trainers but secure much of the technology training through experts in the parent-teacher group. Thus they freed up funds to purchase additional computers to be placed in a lab in the media center that would provide greater accessibility for students and teachers.

CHAPTER 8
Collaboration
in Conflict
Management

GREAT MINDS

"I am prepared to go anywhere, provided it be forward."

DAVID LIVINGSTONE (1813– 1873) This English abolitionist and explorer allowed huge regions of Africa to be mapped and brought major African lakes and Lake Victoria Falls to the attention of Western geographers. A celebrity in Europe and America, Livingstone was barely heard from for six years and is forever associated with the statement, "Dr. Livingstone, I presume," uttered by New York Herald journalist Henry Morton Stanley upon finding him in a remote African town.

While collaborating may be the ideal intervention if there is adequate time and commitment on the part of the parties involved, it is important to note that any of the other styles may be more appropriate in specific situations. For example, when an issue isn't important enough to spend the time required to reach a win-win situation, a compromise may be the best way to settle the conflict.

5. Compromising Compromise enables both parties in a dispute to gain something and lose something. Both parties work out a solution in which each person receives something they want and also gives up something to the other party. Compromise is often used when there is not sufficient time to negotiate for a win-win.

- There were only enough funds available to send one teacher to a national conference and two teachers wanted to attend. The teachers agreed that each of them would get half the funds.

- A parent wanted to give two tickets to teachers to attend a play and four teachers wanted to attend. The teachers agreed that two of them would attend this time and the other two would attend the next time a similar opportunity occurred.

How the Types Respond to Conflict

Two studies have been published on the particular styles the types tend most to use as responses to conflict as shown in figure 8.2.[2, 3] According to these studies, Introverts tend to respond to conflicts initially with avoidance; male ETJ types tend to respond with the competing style. ETJ females along with both extraverted and introverted Thinking and Perceiving types seek compromise. The style of accommodating is the predominant style reported for EFP types. EFJ types report collaboration as their predominant conflict resolution style.

Using Type to Understand and Resolve Conflicts

Our approach to understanding and dealing with conflict is in some measure related to our personality type. When a conflict occurs, our first response around certain issues is to act defensively. We blame others for the conflict and focus on their behaviors. However, examining our own behaviors in a conflict situation is a better place to start in order to understand the conflict and increase our ability to deal with it.

Figure 8.2 *Preferred Conflict Resolution Styles by Personality Type*

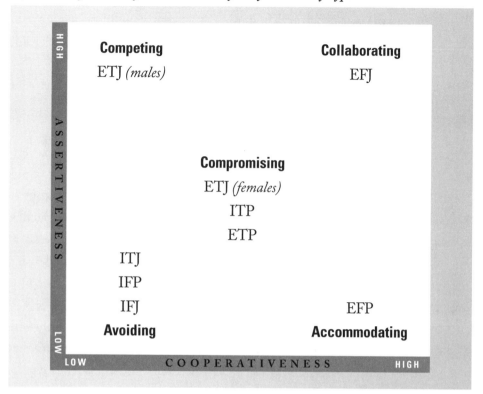

Self-Understanding

When faced with conflict, the following are some questions that we can ask:

- What is my attitude about conflict? Do I believe conflict is negative, stressful, and damaging to relationships? Do I view conflict as a positive force that can provide opportunities to find productive ways of dealing with differences?

- What is my usual approach to solving conflicts? What strategies do I typically use to resolve conflicts? Do I deal with the conflict directly? Avoid dealing with it? Deny that a conflict exists? Try to find a solution that will be mutually satisfying to all parties involved?

- Do I focus on the facts or the specifics of the conflict (i.e., who said what, when, where, what happened?) or the implications and meaning of what happened?

- Do I prefer to focus on the issues related to the conflict or the feelings of those involved in the conflict?

- What type of solutions to conflict do I prefer? Do I prefer solutions that are based on objective criteria? Do I prefer solutions that leave people feeling happy and satisfied and maintain harmony? What do I do when there is disagreement about what seems like a fair solution yet it is one which makes some people unhappy?

Type Differences in Conflict

To understand the type differences in conflict situations, we will consider the preferences individually and then examine how the preferences for Perceiving (Sensing or Intuition) and Judging (Thinking or Feeling) combine with each other. (See Resource 24, *Conflict and Type*.)

Extroversion and Introversion

Extraverts and Introverts approach conflict resolution differently. Extraverts usually want to talk about a conflict right away whereas Introverts prefer to think about the conflict and take some time to consider the issues before discussing it. Because Extraverts enjoy the world of action and interaction and are energized by talking with people, they want to work out differences by talking about them.

Through discussions, Extraverts formulate their ideas and thoughts about the situation. They may not end up where they began because verbalization is an important part of the thinking process they use to arrive at their opinions.

Introverts, on the other hand, are reflective and turn inward when faced with a conflict. They prefer to analyze the situation and reflect inwardly before they share their opinions with others. Because they internalize, others will be unaware of what they are thinking until the Introvert chooses to let them know. When Introverts are frustrated with a situation, they often refuse to talk about it, particularly if they are not certain their viewpoint will be treated with respect.

Because Extraverts want to settle their differences by talking about them, they may be frustrated by Introverts who may avoid discussing the conflict or may stop talking before the conflict has been resolved. Extraverts often assume silence means agreement. For Introverts, silence may simply indicate an unwillingness to reveal what they are thinking or feeling at that moment.

Extraverts can help Introverts by acknowledging their need to reflect and think about the situation. Extraverts may need to stop talking and allow some time for reflection. Introverts can help Extraverts by recognizing their need to talk about a situation. Introverts may need to be more willing to share their reflections. If Introverts choose not to talk at any given moment, they may be willing to tell the Extraverts when they will enter a discussion again.

Sensing and Intuition

Conflict frequently results from differences in perception because Sensing and Intuition types see different aspects of the same situation. Sensing focuses on the facts and details that can be verified. People with a preference for Sensing tend to remember who said what, how long the discussion took, and the body language and facial expressions of the participants.

Because they focus on the present and have a remarkable ability to recall detail and the specific order of events, Sensing types may frustrate Intuitive types who focus on the meaning of the events rather than the details. Because Intuition focuses on the big picture, people with a preference for Intuition may not notice the details or the specific order of events, details that are so important to Sensing types. Rather than remembering things in a step-by-step manner as Sensing types do, Intuitive types respond to the totality of the event. As a result, Intuitive types may be unable to recall the specifics of what happened but are very clear about their overall responses to an event. Sensing types may become frustrated when Intuitive types don't remember some of the specific details that Sensing types feel were an important part of the conflict.

Thinking and Feeling

Thinking types and Feeling types react to conflict and approach conflict resolution very differently due to the different processes they use and their choice of criteria for resolution. Thinking types want to discuss issues from an objective point of view. They want to discuss the realities and the facts, not deal with the personalities involved. Clarifying the differences and looking at things objectively are critical. They want to keep emotions out of the discussions. They search for the equitable thing to do, even if others may be hurt in the process.

Feeling types, on the other hand, usually are uncomfortable with situations that breed discontent and disharmony and may avoid stating what the real concern is for fear of creating ill will or hurting someone. They want people to get along and they strive to create harmony. Their sense of fairness is to consider individual circumstances. They frequently tend to blame themselves for conflicts and will often sacrifice their own comfort to accommodate the other party in order to see a situation resolved. They may feel resentment later, but at the time of the conflict, their emphasis is on removing the differences. Feeling types strive to reach consensus by considering each person's concerns. They want to find a solution that promotes harmony for all.

Many of the conflict situations that occur in schools are a result of differences in the T–F function. Understanding the Thinking type's preference for objectivity and the Feeling type's preference for harmony can serve as a useful tool when conflicts arise.

In working to resolve a conflict with a Feeling type, a person should encourage the expression of feelings and the values that are important in the situation. Ask "What are you feeling right now?" or "What is of most concern to you about this?" Then begin the process of seeking solutions.

For the Thinking type, analyzing the situation and arriving at a logical solution is the best way to solve a conflict. The Thinking type usually wants to talk about the facts, clarify issues, and analyze the situation objectively. Conflicts may arise more frequently over principles. To the Thinking type, objectivity is more important than how people feel.

In discussing a conflict with a Thinking type, one should pay attention to the choice of words used in discussing the conflict. For example, ask "What do you think about this situation?" rather than "How do you feel about the situation?"

Acknowledging feelings first when discussing a conflict with a Feeling type will allow for the validation of those feelings and allows the Feeling type to see that the other person understands something important to him or her. Allowing a Thinking type to express first what is on his or her mind and to explain how the situation was analyzed, results in the Thinking type believing that his or her ideas are respected.

Judging and Perceiving

Judging types and Perceiving types may have difficulty when in conflict with each other due to differences in attitude toward process and closure. Judging types like things planned and organized; they value order and tend to exert control over people, tasks, and the environment. Because of the overriding need to reach closure, they may be frustrated if the Perceiving type resists resolving matters quickly in order to consider more alternatives.

Perceiving types value independence and flexibility and like to keep their options open. Judging types may appear to be overly aggressive and decisive because of their desire to reach closure and move forward to another task.

When confronted with a conflict, Judging types tend to assess the situation and then choose a solution and implement it even if all the information isn't in. Perceiving types tend to regard decisions as tentative and are likely to suggest changing the decision if a better alternative is proposed.

Judging types value closure and may resist attempts at negotiation. Perceiving types value process, are more flexible, and may appear indecisive to others when they are exploring better ways of handling situations. Resource 23, *Type Preferences and Conflict: A Quick Reference Guide*, summarizes these differences.

Paired Functions in Conflict Situations

Considering the preferences individually provides useful information and insight about people's behavior in conflict situations. However, since we use *both* perception (Sensing or Intuition) and judgment (Thinking or Feeling) in actual conflict situations, it is helpful to understand how these functions *combine* to affect behavior.

What follows is information about how people with preferences for Sensing and Thinking (ST), Sensing and Feeling (SF), Intuition and Feeling (NF), and Intuition and Thinking (NT) define and view conflict, react to conflict, and approach its resolution, followed by tips for solving conflicts, as well as examples of applications of this knowledge in a school setting. The four examples are based on an identical situation so that you can clearly see how each preference pair chooses to resolve the conflict.[4]

> **RESOURCES**
>
> RESOURCES 23 and 24 summarize information about type preferences in conflict. RESOURCES 25 through 28 are exercises that can be used with groups to demonstrate type differences in understanding and resolving conflict.[4]

Sensing and Thinking (ST) View of Conflict

ST types view conflict as a situation in which two parties are unable to reach agreement. Opposing ideas or interests frequently cause disagreements and disputes. ST types view conflict as a normal part of life that should be dealt with realistically and practically. Typical sources of conflict for ST types include situations, often practical matters, in which they perceive unfairness, inconsistency, or unresolved issues.

Introverted ST types may tend to withdraw until they have had time to think about ways to deal with a conflict. Extraverted ST types will respond directly and quickly. They will strive to understand the issues involved and try to resolve the problem using logic. They will use an objective analysis in their approach and will want to resolve the conflict as soon as possible. They will seek conflict resolutions that are practical, realistic, workable, efficient, results-oriented, and beneficial to the task or organization.

Approaches to solving conflict. ST types will collect the facts and details, analyze the causes for the conflict, ask questions, and look at the conflict from different points of view. They typically respond directly and objectively and tend not to let emotions interfere in their assessment of the situation or the resolution of the conflict. They like to use a step-by-step, logical approach in their search for a solution: gather the facts and get agreement, analyze the situation objectively, and decide on a solution.

Tips for Solving conflicts with ST types

With preferences for Sensing and Thinking, ST types like to be approached directly when conflict occurs. They respond to a calm, logical approach with an open discussion about the issues. They want others to be open and honest and willing to discuss the conflict. They want to be presented with relevant information and allowed to respond.

STs dislike dealing with those who have not thought through the issues, and they want to be approached calmly and rationally. People who "fly off the handle" with ST types will not receive a positive response!

Example: **An ST Principal's Response to a Conflict Situation**

A teacher brought two boys to the office who had been fighting over whose turn it was to kick the ball in a soccer drill. The ST principal thanked the teacher for bringing the students and said he'd take care of the situation. The principal asked each student to state his side of the situation, listened to them, and asked if they knew the consequences for fighting. Both boys said they knew they would be suspended.

The principal then called the boys' parents, explained what happened, told the parents the boys would be suspended for three days and asked them to come to the school and pick up their children. The principal completed the suspension notices and asked the boys to wait outside his office until their parents arrived.

Sensing and Feeling (SF) View of Conflict

SF types view conflict as a disagreement or problem involving one or more people. Typical sources of conflict for SF types include interpersonal conflicts in which people are taking advantage of other people. SF types tend to see the negative impact conflict has on people and want to find a solution to satisfy everyone involved. They are uncomfortable with conflict and are frequently the "peacemakers" when disagreements occur.

Approaches to solving conflict. Feeling types in general often have an initial reaction to deal with conflict indirectly, either by avoiding confrontation altogether or by accommodating the other person, particularly in a one-on-one conflict. However, when they do engage in conflict management actively, SF types focus on what each person wants so that the conflict can be resolved, encouraging people to talk about their feelings and their views. They are considerate of other's needs and feelings throughout the process of conflict resolution. They show respect, avoid criticizing, treat people kindly, and look for compromises that are acceptable to all involved. Their goals are creating harmony and finding solutions that are agreeable to everyone.

Tips for solving conflicts with SF types

With their preferences for sensing and feeling, SF types like to be approached openly and honestly without blaming when conflict occurs. They will discuss the conflict but want people to be kind and respectful with a willingness to work it out.

Example: An SF Principal's Response to a Conflict Situation

A teacher brought two boys to the office who had been fighting over whose turn it was to kick the ball in a soccer drill. The SF principal told the teacher she appreciated her bringing the boys to the office and said she would take care of the situation. She asked each boy to tell her what led to the fight. She listened attentively and then asked each student to tell her how he might have behaved differently.

She asked the students if they had had any previous difficulties getting along and the boys told her they used to be good friends and frequently played ball together in the neighborhood. She asked them how they settled differences before and then asked if a similar situation occurred again if they thought they could decide whose turn it was without getting into a fight. Both boys assured her they could.

The principal then told the boys she would have to suspend them from school for fighting as the school policy required but hoped in the future they would get along and not get into another fight. She called the boys' parents and told them what happened. She said that although she did not like to suspend students from school she was required to according to school policy. She told the parents that she and the boys had talked and she hoped they had learned to look for ways other than fighting to decide whose turn it was the next time they played soccer together.

Intuition and Feeling (NF) View of Conflict

NF types view conflict as situations in which two or more people have different views on how a situation should be handled. They perceive conflict as stressful to individuals and relationships and thus a negative force. They sometimes see conflict as an opportunity for growth and development so long as it is not at the expense of the relationship. Different needs or opposing ideas, value issues, and communication are frequently sources of conflict for NF types.

Like SF types, NF types may also retreat when confronted with conflict or try to ignore or avoid it. However, they desire harmony and will often contact the person with whom they are in conflict and invite them to try to resolve it. They want situations to be resolved so that each person involved comes away a winner, and they seek creative solutions to make this possible. They encourage input from others, looking for points of agreement as they work with a view towards consensus. They are willing to compromise but may give in too readily rather than risk harming the relationship. Later, they may feel resentful when their own needs are not met.

Approaches to solving conflict. Communication is the key to resolving conflict for NF types, and they encourage input from others and like to hear all sides involved in the conflict. They focus on relationships and will seek creative solutions. They are flexible, cooperative, and willing to compromise. They listen and try to find points of agreement when disagreements occur.

Tips for solving conflicts with NF types

NF types want others to approach them personally when a conflict occurs. They dislike getting impersonal notes. NFs want others to try to understand their side even if others don't agree with it. They like to be approached in a positive, warm, and supportive manner. If a criticism is given, NFs want a strength or positive characteristic mentioned prior to the criticism.

NF types want the focus to be on people with the goal of finding areas of agreement and building or maintaining a harmonious relationship. A willingness to work together to solve the problem is important. NF types like people to be empathic and flexible and willing to be creative in conflict resolution.

Example: An NF Principal's Response to a Conflict Situation

A teacher brought two students to the office who had been fighting over whose turn it was to kick the ball in a soccer drill. The NF principal told the teacher she was sorry there was a fight and said she would talk to the students about the incident.

In her discussion with the boys, she said it was important to learn how to settle differences peacefully and take turns. She said that people can learn to talk out problems together. She listened as each of the students described what happened and then asked them how they might settle their next disagreement without fighting. She told them she hoped they would remember what they had talked about so there would be no more fights the next time they played soccer.

She told the students she was sorry, but the school policy required suspension for fighting and she would have to suspend them. She contacted the students' parents and told them about the incident and their discussion about the negative consequences of fighting. She asked the parents to talk to their children about the importance of getting along with each other and to help them realize that fighting does not solve problems.

Intuition and Thinking (NT) View of Conflict

NT types describe conflict as struggles between opposing ideas or forces or differences in values, ideas, or principles. Conflict occurs when two opposing views occur without acceptance on either side. NT types view conflict as a challenge and an opportunity for innovation and change. Many NT types like conflict and view it as a positive, dynamic force and an inevitable process that ultimately leads to progress. Typical sources of conflict for NT types include matters of principle, disagreement over priorities, and taking on too many responsibilities. Conflict also occurs over miscommunication and differences in perception.

NT types enjoy problem solving and will often respond directly when a conflict occurs. They enjoy the challenge of finding ways to resolve conflict and use their intuition to create innovative solutions. They analyze the situation, ask questions, and clarify the issues. They can also be argumentative. They may be stubborn and unwilling to change their positions, especially if it involves a matter of principle; they may end up agreeing to disagree.

Approaches to solving conflict. NT types consider the pros and cons of the situation and use reasoning and logic in searching for a solution. They use a problem-solving approach and tend to remain objective and avoid personalizing the issues. They may involve others, listen to all sides, and encourage an open, honest exchange of ideas.

Tips for solving conflicts with NT types

With their preferences for Intuition and Thinking, NT types like to be approached directly and in a calm and rational manner. They value openness and honesty and a willingness to try a new and different approach to conflict resolution. NT types are strategists and want others to be willing to strategize and consider numerous alternatives before selecting the best solution to implement.

Example: An NT Principal's Response to a Conflict Situation

A teacher brought two boys to the principal's office who were involved in a fight over whose turn it was to kick the soccer ball in a drill. The NT principal thanked the teacher for bringing the students to the office and said she would take care of the situation. She asked each student to explain what happened from his point of view while the other one listened. She asked the students if they thought fighting was the best way to resolve their difference over whose turn it was to kick the ball or if there were other ways they might have decided the issue without a fight.

The boys suggested several different approaches they might have taken such as a coin toss, drawing straws, or asking their teacher to pick a number and the boy who guessed a number closest to it would get to kick the soccer ball first. The principal stated that in the future she hoped they would use more creative approaches to problem solving instead of getting into a fight. She told them they would both be suspended according to school board policy and then called their parents to let them know.

Working collaboratively to manage conflict, while presenting new challenges for principals and teachers, offers the rewards of higher morale and greater motivation, increased administrative support, new ideas, best practices, and higher student achievement. It's not a bad investment!

- Managing and mediating conflict is a major aspect of problem solving.
- Conflict is viewed differently according to type preferences.
- Most ways of responding to conflict can be categorized into five categories:
    - Avoiding
    - Accommodating
    - Competing
    - Collaborating
    - Compromising
- Our approach to understanding and dealing with conflict is in some measure related to our personality type:
    - Extraverts usually want to talk about a conflict right away.
    - Introverts prefer to think about the conflict and take some time to consider the issues before discussing it.
- Conflict frequently results from differences in perception or judgment:
    - Sensing types remember specifics and focus on the facts of the current situation.
    - Intuitives focus on patterns and interpret the meaning of the situation rather than the details.
    - Thinking types want to discuss the issues from an objective point of view and seek an equitable resolution.
    - Feeling types strive for harmony and seek a resolution based on individual circumstances. They tend to blame themselves for conflicts.
- Many of the conflict situations in schools are a result of differences in the T–F function
- Understanding the Thinking preference for objectivity and the Feeling preference for interpersonal or intrapersonal harmony can serve as a useful tool when conflicts arise.

- Judging types value order and structure. They tend to assess the situation, choose a solution, and implement it.
- Perceiving types tend to regard possible solutions to conflicts as tentative and may suggest changing the solution if a better alternative is proposed. They value independence and flexibility and like to keep their options open.

Check Your Understanding

Q *How do ST types view conflict?*

A ST types view conflict as a situation in which two parties are unable to reach agreement. They like to use a step-by-step, logical approach to solving conflicts and in their search for a solution.

Q *How do SF types view conflict?*

A SF types view conflict as a disagreement or problem involving one or more people. They do not like conflict and want to solve it so everyone is comfortable with the solution. They want to be approached openly and honestly without blaming when conflict occurs. They will discuss the conflict but want everyone to be respectful with a willingness to work things out.

Q *How do NF types view conflict?*

A NF types view conflict as stressful and as situations in which two or more people have different views on how a situation should be handled. They like to be approached in a positive, warm, and supportive manner. They want the focus to be on people with the goal of finding areas of agreement and building or maintaining a harmonious relationship.

Q *How do NT types view conflict?*

A NT types view conflict as struggles between opposing ideas or forces or differences in values, ideas, or principles. They enjoy problem solving and will use reason and logic in searching for a solution. They like to be approached directly and in a rational manner and want others to be willing to strategize and consider alternative solutions to the conflict.

Q *What are five conflict resolution styles?*

A Five conflict resolution styles are avoiding, accommodating, competing, compromising and collaborating.

Q *Read the following scenario and categorize the conflict resolution styles, according to the approaches from which Mrs. Stuart might choose.*

Scenario: Several students in Mrs. Adams' algebra class told Mrs. Stuart, the student council advisor, that Mrs. Adams had scheduled a big unit test the day of Homecoming. The students knew they would be up late the night before preparing for the event and were concerned they would not have time to study for the test and also knew they would be tired on the day the test was scheduled. They asked Mrs. Stuart to talk to Mrs. Adams about postponing the test until Monday. Mrs. Stuart could take several different approaches to handling the students' request.

1) She could tell the students she did not want to get involved and didn't want to talk to Mrs. Adams.

2) She could ask Mrs. Adams to allow the students to take the test on Monday and if she agreed tell her she would do her lunch duty.

3) She could go to Mrs. Adams and talk about the situation and try to work out a solution so Mrs. Adams and the students were both happy.

4) She could tell Mrs. Adams it was unfair of her to schedule a test the day of one of the biggest events of the school year and tell her if she didn't change the test date she would go to the principal and ask him to make her change it.

5) She could try to get Mrs. Adams to allow the students to take the test at an earlier time convenient to her in exchange for the students assisting her in some way.

A

1) Avoiding

2) Accommodating

3) Collaborating

4) Competing

5) Compromising

- How do you view conflict? What strategies do you typically use to resolve conflicts?

- Think about a recent conflict situation you've experienced and your response. Categorize your response according to the conflict resolution style you used.

- Think about a recent conflict situation you know about. Categorize the responses of the persons involved according to the conflict resolution styles used. If you know the people's types, how are their types indicative of their responses to the conflict?

CHAPTER 8

Collaboration

in Conflict

Management

9

Collaboration in School Operations

Collaboration among colleagues is a means to an end:
enhancing teaching and learning.

ALAN M. BLANKSTEIN, *Failure is Not an Option*

Collaboration is essential for effective leadership of today's complex schools. Collaboration is also needed in the day-to-day operation of schools. School principals have the ultimate responsibility for managing the entire school organization and are expected to do so efficiently and effectively, all the while inspiring staff and students to perform at their best. Managing the operation of a school is no easy task! Principals' tasks and responsibilities include establishing an environment that is safe, productive, and enjoyable; hiring teachers and other school personnel; providing support and materials; and evaluating staff performance.

Principals must also manage school finances, supervise the maintenance of the building and grounds, oversee the grading and reporting of student performance, coordinate the numerous school activities and special events, and handle myriad other tasks necessary for the smooth operation of the school. In virtually all of these areas type knowledge can be applied to help others work collaboratively and effectively in the daily operation of a school.

In this chapter, we provide information and practical tips for the daily operation of schools, using the following specific applications of personality type to illustrate and demonstrate effective ways of working with people and getting the work done:

- Recognizing people for their achievements and accomplishments
- Giving support and encouragement
- Considering type differences when determining responsibility for tasks

- Approaching people about accepting a task or assuming a responsibility
- Handling disagreements and difficulties
- Improving meetings
- Improving the work environment

Recognizing Achievements and Accomplishments

People perform at their highest levels when they feel good about themselves and possess high levels of confidence. In *Wired for Conflict*, author VanSant wrote "Confidence and a sense of well-being come from both self-acceptance and from knowing we have done good work. The latter typically emerges from beginning a process with our natural preferences and then using those opposite parts of our minds that require more intentional effort."[1]

Almost everyone appreciates being recognized for their achievements and accomplishments. We enjoy confidence and a sense of well-being when we know we have done a good job. Yet workplace surveys consistently indicate that recognition and appreciation is an area most often short-changed or given inappropriately by organizational managers. The Thinking–Feeling dichotomy is particularly sensitive in this arena, especially in timing and in the form recognition takes.

Significance of Thinking and Feeling Differences

People with a preference for Thinking generally associate productivity with result or product. Those with this preference typically want to be recognized for their work *after* a project or task is completed. They tend to view compliments or acknowledgments of their work prior to completion of the project as irrelevant and unnecessary, perhaps even insincere and patronizing. They want to be thanked when the project is completed. A valuable and meaningful way to recognize a Thinking type would be to say, "The end of the year celebration was a big success! Everyone is talking about how well it went and how much they enjoyed it! Thank you for your hard work. We really appreciate all you did to make the event such a big success!"

People with a Feeling preference, on the other hand, associate productivity with both personal involvement and the product. People with this preference often want to be recognized for their productivity in a personal way and typically want appreciation for their *effort* as well as for successful completion of a task. They value and appreciate being thanked and their contributions acknowledged *throughout* the process of working on a task or project. Occasional positive feedback all the way through the process maintains and increases motivation.

"I know the price of success: dedication, hard work, and an unremitting devotion to the things you want to see happen."

FRANK LLOYD WRIGHT (1867–1959) This Wisconsin-born architect ushered in a distinctive American architectural style specializing in residential and public structures that harmonized design with landscape and form with function.

For example, a meaningful way to show appreciation to a Feeling type would be to say, "I have noticed how hard you are working to get ready for the end of the year celebration and really appreciate all you are doing. I know the event will be a big success because of your dedication and effort. Thank you for giving your time and energy to this important event." This comment acknowledges the person's effort during the process of preparing for the event and may motivate the person to work even harder! Of course, appreciation and recognition need to be shown following successful completion of the event as well.

Preference for the form recognition takes varies by type. All people feel recognized and appreciated with the reward of a promotion, salary increase, or bonus. Unfortunately, education does not often lend itself to this kind of compensation for a job well done! However, understanding the Thinking and Feeling functions as Judging functions that significantly contribute to how a person assesses his or her self-worth provides information school administrators *do* have available to appropriately recognize and thus motivate their staff.

Thinking types value verbal feedback that concisely explains why their project or product is worthy of recognition. The suggestion given above would be even more valued if a few specifics were included. ("The end-of-year event was fun, attracted the largest number of participants we've ever had, was well-organized, and offered something for everybody.") Thinking types may vary (perhaps by Extraversion and Introversion preferences) as to whether they want the recognition written or verbal or whether they want to be recognized publicly or just personally. However, the most valued recognition focuses directly on the result or product.

Feeling types will often respond positively to symbolic as well as direct recognition and appreciate flowers, candy, lunch treats, or a personal hand-written note.

CHAPTER 9
Collaboration
in School
Operations

One example illustrating type differences occurred in a workshop we conducted for educators. With participants placing themselves in either the Thinking or Feeling group, we asked how they wanted to be recognized for a successful project. The Thinking group was adamant about wanting to be recognized for their competence. For them, a compliment meant acknowledging specific characteristics that made the project successful.

The Feeling group on the other hand, wanted the compliment to be more personal. They loved getting flowers or candy in recognition of success. They said they enjoyed getting, for example, Hershey Kisses in their mail box on Teacher Appreciation Day.

The Thinking group was almost aghast that the Feeling group could feel good about receiving candy kisses, which the Thinking types regarded almost as an insult! They wanted another form of recognition such as a memo for their personnel file or a personal one-on-one acknowledgement of their achievement. The Feeling group acknowledged they would appreciate this type of recognition as well—it just had not occurred to them! A summary of the differences between how Thinking types and Feeling types like to be recognized is shown in figure 9.1.[2]

Figure 9.1 *Differences Between How Thinking and Feeling Types Like to Be Recognized*

Thinking (T)	Feeling (F)
• Wants recognition/appreciation for a task well done when the task is completed • Tends to discount or find irrelevant appreciation given for effort during the process of task completion • Values recognition most when it is focused on the task and contains specifics	• Wants appreciation for their personal involvement and effort as well as recognition for a task well done. • Feels most highly motivated when appreciation is given at appropriate times throughout a project or task. • Values symbolic expressions of appreciation as well as task-focused expressions

This differentiation is easier to make when a principal knows the preferences of a staff member. Often this is not the case, of course. The wonderful thing about personality type is that people usually know the preferred behaviors of their type even if they do not know the type "labels" for their mental functioning.

The "short-hand" of type talk may not be available to the conversation, but a principal can outline the various ways people like to receive feedback without using the labels. Then at some point, the principal can check in with staff on a personal basis to find out what they like to be recognized for and when they like to receive this recognition. Follow-through on this is virtually a guaranteed staff morale booster! Resource 29, *Recognition and Appreciation by Type*, provides an activity that can be used to help people describe how they prefer to be recognized and appreciated.

Giving Support and Encouragement

Certainly teachers and others who work in schools may frequently experience difficult situations. An upset parent may confront a teacher and challenge her authority and teaching ability; a student may make rude and unkind remarks to a teacher; a class may become unruly and refuse to cooperate; a teacher may have spent a great deal of time planning for a unit of instruction only to find it didn't work out as intended; faculty members may have disagreements; and of course, personal and family demands can place additional stress on already overworked teachers. Support and encouragement are needed in each of these situations.

In a caring school, people support and encourage each other when difficulties occur. They reach out and try to help when things go wrong. People respond to difficult situations in different ways, many of them type related. When people want to give support and encouragement it is helpful for them to understand the different expressions of type preferences and to know the best way to give support and encouragement to someone of a particular preference.

Typical ways the preferences are expressed and specific tips for giving people support and encouragement are provided in figure 9.2.

GREAT MINDS

"Words empty as the wind are best left unsaid."

HOMER (Before 700 B.C.) Legend records Homer as a blind Greek poet who wrote down the epic poems, *The Iliad* and *The Odyssey*. The concepts in these works set the basic worldview of ancient Greeks and represent the oldest surviving works of European literature.

Figure 9.2 *Ways to Give Support*

Extraverts (E)	Introverts (I)
• Will want to talk about a concern or situation. • Will work their way to a solution as they talk—(first comments are not usually their final conclusions). **Tips:** • Invite them to talk about the situation and listen to them without interrupting. • Expect some change of direction as new information or ideas emerge in the course of discussion.	• Will want to think through concerns before talking about them. • May tend to keep their concerns inside and not want to talk—until they have decided what to do about the situation. **Tips:** • Give them time to gather their thoughts before expecting them to talk about the situation. • Invite them to share their thoughts and be attentive even if there are periods of silence.
Sensing (S) Types	**Intuitive (N) Types**
• Will be concerned about the practicality and reality of the situation. • Will talk about specifics and give lots of details. **Tips:** • If asked, give them concrete, practical, and realistic suggestions. • Be concise and clear when making statements.	• Will be concerned about implications and meaning of the situation. • Will talk about the big picture and may not be clear about the details. **Tips:** • If asked, give them an overview of several possible actions. • Couch these suggestions in terms of options.
Thinking (T) Types	**Feeling (F) Types**
• Will analyze the situation in a rational and objective manner. **Tips:** • Encourage them to talk about what they think. • Be logical and concise.	• Will be concerned about the personal impact on people. **Tips:** • Encourage them to talk about how they feel in the situation. • Be empathic.

Figure 9.2 *continued*

Judging (J) Types	Perceiving (P) Types
• Will want to take decisive action and bring closure to the situation.	• Will want to keep options open as long as possible.
Tips:	**Tips:**
• Encourage them to share possible solutions and help them arrive at decisions and actions they can take.	• Encourage them to share alternative possibilities for handling the situation.
• Focus on bringing closure but help them not push for a final decision if more information is needed.	• Focus on keeping options open and not rushing to a decision but help them commit to a deadline if this is needed for the situation at hand.

Determining Responsibility for Tasks

An effective strategy to determine responsibility for tasks is to consider type preferences and give people choices when assigning tasks and responsibilities. Tasks and responsibilities can be delegated based on type preferences. Allowing people to select which tasks they prefer allows them to perform tasks that are related to their strengths and interests.

Figure 9.3 shows examples of the types of tasks that administrators, teachers, and team members often prefer by type. The list is useful for identifying preferred tasks and is helpful for understanding why some people perform and like certain tasks better than others. Certainly people cannot always be assigned their preferred tasks, but it is helpful to know the types of tasks people may prefer when given a choice.

GREAT MINDS

"Tact is the art of making a point without making an enemy."

ISAAC NEWTON (1642–1727) In one of the great landmarks of scientific history, this English physicist and mathematician explained the motion of falling bodies on earth and in the solar system using calculus, a field of mathematics which he developed.

Figure 9.3 *Tasks Preferred by the Types*

Sensing and Thinking (ST)	
• Collecting facts and information.	• Organizing information.
• Preparing agendas.	• Developing timelines for task completion.
• Short-term projects requiring physical or technical skills, e.g., building a sound booth, creating a butterfly garden, installing picnic benches and tables on campus.	• Managing a budget for a special project or for the school.
• Organizing the distribution of materials and supplies.	• Making assignments to individuals.
• Outlining plans for completion of tasks.	• Developing action plans to implement new programs.
• Designing the schedule of teachers to classes.	• Making room assignments to teachers.
Sensing and Feeling (SF)	
• Helping teachers who have difficulty with students.	• Compiling survey results from teachers, students, and parents if they are interested in the purpose of the survey.
• Serving on a teacher appreciation committee.	• Developing guidelines to help students with special needs.
• Organizing or working on school activities and special events.	• Assigning students to teachers.

Figure 9.3 *continued*

Intuition and Feeling (NF)	
• Helping teachers with difficult students.	• Creating programs to recognize teachers and students.
• Creating new activities and instructional programs to benefit students.	• Designing special events for students.
• Developing new curriculum.	• Ordering special items to give to teachers and students.
• Developing and conducting staff development programs or activities.	

Intuition and Thinking (NT)	
• Designing new programs and activities.	• Analyzing data.
• Developing a system for a process or procedure.	• Designing school improvement plans.
• Leading the development of new policies and procedures.	• Problem solving.
• Developing new curriculum.	• Developing policies.

Approaching People About Accepting a Task or Responsibility

We believe type differences provide useful information to enable us to approach people about accepting a particular task or responsibility they will find compatible. Some examples of tasks and responsibilities compatible with type preferences are outlined in table 9.a (page 162).

GREAT MINDS

"A pessimist sees the difficulty in every opportunity; an optimist sees the opportunity in every difficulty."

WINSTON CHURCHILL (1874–1965) Britain's World War II-period prime minister led his nation to victory against Nazi Germany deploying eloquence and determination to inspire the people of his beleaguered island.

Table 9.a

Extraversion	Extraverts are often comfortable speaking in front of an audience and can be the "spokesperson" for a committee or proposed plan. They could be asked to make a presentation at a parent-teacher meeting explaining the proposed changes to the daily schedule.
Introversion	Introverts often enjoy doing research and putting ideas in writing. They could be asked to prepare the written report from the committee studying a later school starting time or to design an orientation program for new teachers to help them become familiar with the school.
Sensing	Sensing types will often provide structure and sequence of tasks or provide creative ways to adapt something that already exists to accomplish a goal. They could be asked to prepare an outline of the action steps required for the implementation of the new science curriculum or suggest action-oriented ways for introducing the new curriculum.
Intuition	Intuitive types are often creative, innovative, and enjoy learning new skills and designing new procedures and programs. They could be asked to be involved in designing a new orientation program for fifth graders who are getting ready to enter middle school for the first time.
Thinking	Thinking types like analytical problem solving and are typically comfortable taking charge of a project, group, or development of an idea. They could be asked to chair a task force to find a solution for the recurring issue of students arriving late to class.
Feeling	Feeling types are concerned about how an action affects people and also like to learn new skills and design or implement new procedures and programs. They could be included on a committee to design a new program to help students who are struggling in math.
Judging	Judging types are purposeful and plan well. They like to work towards a goal and strive for task-completion. They could be included on the committee to recommend changes to the third-grade reading program and asked to develop a timeline for implementation of the recommended changes.
Perceiving	Perceiving types are open and receptive to changes and generally are flexible, adaptable and spontaneous. They could be included on any committee where spontaneity and flexibility are needed.

Certainly, preference does not necessarily equal performance and given a choice, staff members may sometimes select tasks that allow them to "flex" to their less-preferred functions for a variety of reasons including the desire to increase their skills in that function. Principals and others will also out of necessity need to approach people from time to time to undertake a particular task that may be outside their preferences.

Handling Disagreements and Difficulties

When people have disagreements or do not seem to be working together well, quite often the situation can be understood in light of type differences. To begin working towards a solution, the individuals or the team can first discuss what is happening by translating differences into possible type differences. This approach helps to depersonalize the issues and may support better group dynamics through the accommodation of type differences. Resolving differences related to type often goes more smoothly than other interpersonal issues. Untangling the type issues is a good first step to working through other underlying problems.

Type theory implies that there are some disagreements that can be anticipated simply from type differences. Following are some typical examples:

- An Extravert is not giving an Introvert enough time to reflect before expecting a response.
- An Introvert is not willing to share his or her thoughts and ideas.
- A Sensing type insists on having all the specifics when what the Intuitive has is a "good idea."
- A Feeling type believes a Thinking type is not showing enough concern for people and relationships.
- A Thinking type believes a Feeling type prefers harmony at the expense of a fair resolution to the problem.
- A Judging type wants to bring closure without allowing the Perceiving type sufficient time to present additional information or alternatives.
- A Perceiving type wants to consider additional options when the Judging type feels a decision must be made.

When people whose personality types are different are asked to work together on a project, their approaches to the completion of the project and their manner of working on it are also likely to be different. Team members can discuss these differences and acknowledge their impact on the working relationship. They can recognize the role type differences can play and learn to appreciate the strengths each partner brings to the project.

The following case study is a brief illustration of how two people used their knowledge of type to understand their differences, and, as a result, increased their effectiveness as team members.

Barbara (an ESTJ) and Peggy (an INFP) were asked to serve as co-chairpersons of the school improvement team. In their roles as co-chairpersons they had the responsibility of leading the school effort to bring about changes to improve the school. The school improvement team had to develop a three-year plan that included developing mission and vision statements, goals and objectives, strategies, and activities, as well as a timeline to implement the plan. The team had regular meetings and the co-chairpersons developed the agendas for the meetings.

Barbara thought they should complete the task of developing the school improvement plan as quickly and efficiently as possible, sticking to the agenda and without a great deal of time spent socializing. She saw no reason to have refreshments unless the meetings were to last longer than an hour.

Peggy wanted members of the school improvement team to have time to get to know each other and build relationships as they discussed the strengths and weaknesses of the school and developed the school improvement plan. She wanted team members to have time to reflect on the current situation and to discuss many possibilities for changes and recommendations. Peggy (the INFP) was frustrated when Barbara (the ESTJ) attempted to restrict the discussions by focusing on the practicality of the ideas and reminding members of the need to "stick to the agenda" and complete the task in a timely fashion.

While willing to allow some time for brainstorming ideas, Barbara became frustrated when the discussions were prolonged and appeared to be "off target." Peggy wanted the team to consider many options and most importantly make certain that all members of the committee contributed to the discussion and felt their contributions were valued. She wanted the team to be flexible and enjoy spontaneous discussions of topics tangentially related to the topics on the agenda.

CHAPTER 9
Collaboration
in School
Operations

By recognizing their differences and discussing them openly, the co-chairpersons learned to better understand each other. As a result, they were able to use their knowledge of type to design ways to work together effectively and were successful at using their respective areas of strength.

For example, Barbara assumed responsibility for preparing the agendas for the school improvement team meetings and made certain the team followed the agenda. Peggy was attentive to the needs of the team members and made certain they were involved and felt their contributions were valued. The co-chairpersons agreed they would have refreshments and a time for socializing within a set period at the beginning of their meetings and would end the meetings at the agreed upon time.

Because they discussed their type preferences, Peggy (INFP) realized the importance to Barbara (ESTJ) of staying on task in order to develop the school improvement plan as efficiently as possible by the deadline. Barbara realized the importance to Peggy of being flexible and open to new ideas and the value of harmony on the team and making members feel their contributions were valued.

Although the development of the school improvement plan may have taken longer than anticipated, the quality of the plan was significantly better because of the openness and positive relationships developed among the co-chairpersons and team members, which allowed them to present and evaluate ideas effectively and reach consensus for a well-developed plan.

When difficulties occur in the work environment and people get off task or procrastinate and things are bogged down, one way we can work together to establish a productive dialogue is by understanding and honoring type differences. Making constructive use of our knowledge of the innate differences in the way we use our mental processes allows us to take more conscious control of ourselves in situations where differences occur in order to work collaboratively with people.

Figure 9.4 *Provides some suggestions for approaching the different types in ways that can increase the effective handling of differences.*

ST Types	Give Sensing and Thinking types specific details and examples and then state the concern. **Example:** *"It's great that twenty-six of your students are at or above grade level. There are four students in your class who are testing below grade level. We need to figure out how to engage those students as well."*
SF Types	Give Sensing and Feeling types specific details and then ask them to help. **Example:** *"Congratulations! Twenty-six of your students are at or above grade level. We need to help the four students who are still below grade level. Can you think of some ways to make that happen?"*
NF Types	Give Intuition and Feeling types a chance to cooperate with you on a common concern. **Example:** *"Most of your students are performing up to or above expectations. Congratulations! How can we work together to reach those who aren't?"*
NT Types	Give Intuition and Thinking types an overall assessment first and then give them specific details and examples to illustrate the concern. **Example:** *"Most of your students are successful this year and are working at or above grade level. The challenge is to reach those who are not. What do you suggest?"*

Tip: When discussing differences with Feeling types listen for and acknowledge how they are personally experiencing the situation; this approach allows for the validation of the values underlying the feelings. Once Feeling types believe the other person understands something important to them, then they can move more easily into a problem-solving mode.

Example: *"I can hear how tough it is to have to share classroom space with another teacher. It's certainly not the best situation. Any ideas how we can work it out differently?"*

Tip: When discussing differences with a Thinking type, acknowledge first what's on their minds. This approach allows for the validation of the Thinking Types' ideas and analysis of the situation and they will believe their ideas are valued.

Example: *"It sounds like you've given a lot of thought to a difficult situation. What are some alternatives?"*

Improving Meetings

Many people will tell you they dislike going to meetings. However, these same people will also let you know when they have been to a good meeting. Typically they will say the meeting was well-planned and organized and everyone had an opportunity to be involved in the discussion. They will say the meeting started and ended on time, there was a written agenda, the leader stuck to the agenda and time was used well. Some tips for successful meetings include having agendas, establishing ground rules, using an "issues bin," and considering "rounds" when a long discussion is needed. Following are some details about using these methods.

Agendas

Prepare a written agenda for the meeting. Whenever possible distribute the agenda prior to the meeting and have extra copies available as people enter the meeting.

Introverts like to have the agenda *before* the meeting so they will have time to review it. They also generally prefer minimal deviation from the agenda once the meeting is underway. Extraverts want an agenda but often give it attention only as they come into the meeting unless they are going to be asked to give a thoughtful response to a topic or issues. As the agenda unfolds, Extraverts may seem to Introverts like moving targets changing direction unexpectedly in a discussion. Usually this is an example of Extraverts in action—talking out ideas as new information emerges, even if these new ideas are not on the agenda!

Establish Norms

It is important to establish norms for a meeting and involve participants in determining these norms. (Examples of possible norms include everyone agrees to participate; everyone agrees to listen to and respect each other; no sarcastic comments or put downs; if someone is having difficulty with an idea, it's okay to voice the concern; it's okay to ask for additional information or clarification if you don't understand something; wild ideas are welcome—they can be tamed later!) Once the norms are decided upon, everyone should agree to follow them!

Since desired norms vary by type, it is important that participants are involved in determining the norms. For instance, Extraverts like to brainstorm verbally and Introverts like to reflect on their ideas internally. Both discussion and reflection time may be important to the group. People with a preference for Intuition like to work with big picture ideas; people with a preference for Sensing like to know what the supporting data is. Remember to build in norms that accommodate all the preferences.

An important dynamic often overlooked is a difference between Thinking and Feeling that sometimes occurs. A solution reached by the group may not "sit right" with someone with a preference for Feeling, yet that person may not be able to explain immediately why this is so. It is possible this indicates that the solution conflicts with a value important to the person with a Feeling preference. Unlike logical reasons that can often be identified quickly, it may take some time for a personal value to be identified. If a Feeling type agrees with the logic of the solution, but it is contrary to one of their values then he or she may have difficulty with "buy in" later. Therefore, it may be important for the group to build in a norm that, unless a decision is absolutely necessary at that moment, it is appropriate for anyone to ask that a decision be postponed or revisited later to allow reflective time.

These same phenomena can happen for a Thinking type whose Feeling values may be in conflict with the decision. The difference is that logic often outweighs the discomfort and the moment passes. Using the Z decision-making model (see Resource 21) can help to ensure discussion of both the logic and person-centered values.

The leader of the meeting should allow time for discussion *and* reflection as people present new ideas and suggestions. If there is no need to make a decision immediately, it may be wise to table the decision and allow people time to think about what was discussed and make the decision at a later meeting.

Use an "Issues Bin"

The "issues bin" is a strategy to gather additional ideas, questions, and related concerns and to help ensure that everyone has an opportunity to share views and opinions. Group leaders provide a flip chart and sticky notes to the participants, who are encouraged to write thoughts, ideas, questions, and things to consider on the sticky notes and then place them on the flip chart. The "issues bin" is set up in a corner of the meeting room and is available for participants throughout the meeting.

This strategy of using an "issues bin" allows participants to add issues that need to be addressed without interrupting the flow of the meeting. Following completion of the meeting, the notes are typed and shared so that everyone at the meeting can review the comments and consider them in the follow-up discussions.

Extraverts often like this arrangement because it allows them to be able to ask their questions, make their points, or share their concerns at the time they occur to them even if they don't say them aloud. Introverts also like this technique as it provides them with an opportunity to ask a question or make their points, or share concerns more privately.

Consider Rounds for Topics Needing Lengthy Discussion

Extraverts and Introverts often require different amounts of conversation about a topic. Leaders of meetings can establish the time frame for rounds of discussions on particular topics. Once a decision is made as to the length of a round, it is important to stick to it and then agree on another time for the next round. This may be particularly useful with conflict situations.

Improving the Work Environment

In chapter 3, "Personalizing the Learning Environment," we discussed ways to ensure the type preferences for the learning environment are addressed for students. These preferences are also relevant for the working environment of adults in the school. For example, "Introverts generally want quiet and minimal distracting activity to do their best work. Extraverts often need this environment as well when they need to concentrate. However, they also need frequent access to external activity in order to keep their energy and motivation high."[3]

Thinking types prefer an orderly, businesslike environment where people are treated equitably. Feeling types like a warm and friendly environment where people are treated kindly and care and concern for others are demonstrated.

Sensing types work best in an environment that is orderly and conducive to focusing on something specific. Intuitives work best in an environment that encourages creativity.

Judging types work best in an organized environment with clear expectations where they can structure their activities. Perceiving types are likely to organize their environment in a less structured fashion.

Perhaps the most useful tip of all to enable us to work effectively with others is to let others know our own needs respectfully and clearly. For example, it is best to say, "What is happening here is important to me. For me to give it my best shot and fully participate, I need . . . " Also remember to ask what the other person needs: "I think we both want what is best here. What do you need in order to give it your best shot and fully participate?"

Although some of the answers may not be type related, most likely they will be authentic and genuine responses. By looking for type cues, though, we can make the required shift to our less-preferred functions, which can provide the opportunity to connect with others in a more efficient and meaningful manner.

Collaborative leadership in school operations, while presenting new challenges as people work together, offers many rewards, such as better decisions, solutions to problems, management of conflict, improvements in school operations, and benefits to students. It's not a bad investment!

Some ways to apply personality type in the daily operation of schools:

- Recognize people and show appreciation:
  - Thinking types prefer to be recognized after a project is completed.
  - Feeling types prefer to be appreciated during the course of the project as well as upon completion.
- Give support and encouragement:
  - Let Extroverts talk about a concern.
  - Let Introverts have time to gather their thoughts before they talk about their concern.
  - Be clear and concise when making suggestions to a Sensing type.
  - Frame suggestions to Intuitive types in terms of possibilities.
  - Encourage Judging types to share possible solutions and focus on bringing closure.
  - Focus on keeping options open but help Perceiving types commit to a deadline if needed.
- Consider type preferences when determining responsibility for tasks or approaching people about accepting a task or responsibility.
- When disagreements and difficulties occur analyze the situation according to type differences:
  - When discussing differences with a Feeling type listen for and acknowledge how they are personally experiencing the situation and thus allow for the validation of the values underlying the feelings.
  - When discussing differences with a Thinking type, acknowledge first what's on their minds and allow for the validation of their ideas and analysis of the situation.

- Ways to improve meetings:
  - Prepare a written agenda.
  - Establish ground rules.
  - Gather additional suggestions and concerns by using an "issues bin."
  - Consider rounds for topics needing long discussion.
- People perform best when their work environment accommodates their type preferences.

Check Your Understanding

Scenario: Rebecca spent countless hours planning and organizing the annual Spring Festival for the school. She really appreciated the weekly meetings with the principal in which she provided updates on the progress she was making and made him aware of any specific needs she had or difficulties that she was facing in getting ready for the event. After each of these meetings she felt appreciated and was happy she had agreed to take on this major responsibility. When the event was over and a big success the principal sent her flowers and praised her in front of the entire staff.

Q *Does Rebecca have a preference for Thinking or Feeling?*

A Rebecca probably has a preference for Feeling. She enjoyed being complimented as she worked on the planning and loved receiving the flowers as a form of appreciation for her hard work.

Scenario: The principal wanted the school to host an International Night in which students from other countries who attended the school would be able to share information about their cultures. He thought students, teachers, and parents would benefit from preparing for and participating in such an event.

Q *How could the principal use his knowledge of type to approach people about working on the committee responsible for planning the International Night?*

A The principal could try to include people of various types on the committee. For example, he could ask a person with preferences for Sensing and Thinking (ST) since this person would likely enjoy handling many of the practical aspects of the festival and would be very detail oriented. He could ask a person with preferences for Sensing and Feeling (SF) since this person would likely enjoy helping with the organizational details and would also develop ways for everyone to feel welcome and included. He could ask a person with preferences for Intuition and Thinking (NT) since this person would likely enjoy designing the activity and developing procedures for the event and would be helpful in solving any problems that occurred. He could ask a person with preferences for Intuition and Feeling (NF) since this person would also enjoy creating the special features of the event and would find ways for students and adults to benefit from attending the event and would strive to ensure everyone involved had a positive experience.

Getting Started

- Try at least one type-related suggestion to improve the process when you have your next meeting.

- Be aware of the work environments that the different types prefer and strive to ensure the preferred environment is in place. When someone is having difficulty with the work environment introduce one type-related change.

- Be sensitive to the differences between Extraverts and Introverts when a problem or difficult situation occurs. Note these differences with one other person whose preference for Extraversion or Introversion is different from yours. Look for opportunity to accommodate their preference.

GREAT MINDS

"Any book that helps a child to form a habit of reading, to make reading one of his deep and continuing needs, is good for him."

MAYA ANGELOU (born Marguerite Ann Johnson, 1928) This American writer and poet broke down barriers for black women in the arts with the publication of her autobiography, *I Know Why the Caged Bird Sings*. Her stardom soared after she read one of her poems during the 1993 inauguration ceremony of President Bill Clinton.

10
Introducing Type in Schools

An important step in introducing type into an organization is to find out the goal that the knowledge of type is intended to serve; the members' clarity about the goal; and their commitment to achieving it.

GORDON LAWRENCE
People Types and Tiger Stripes

Getting started with type in schools involves a solid knowledge of type, experience, connections, a convincing case for typology as a useful tool, and sheer grit! Schools are inundated every year with additional demands including new programs, new requirements, and new accountability issues. School personnel understandably have an aversion to giving up precious time and energy for yet one more new idea when they are already overextended and have many demands on their time.

At the same time, teachers and administrators, who have incorporated type into their work, report substantial increase in achievement, morale, and greater accomplishment of their educational goals. So how can you capture the audience of educators in order to welcome the entry of type into a school?

Opportunities for learning about type and the benefits of introducing type into schools are numerous. For instance, you might interest a local newspaper in running an article on type, or you could provide programs for civic clubs and neighborhood associations to stimulate interest in psychological type. An individual teacher, counselor, or administrator may attend a workshop, be very enthusiastic, and want others in their school to learn about type. Educational leadership programs run by states, departments of education, or school districts may include information about type and opportunities for follow up in schools. Parents and educators may learn about type through parent-teacher associations, public library forums, home schooling associations, or other organizations. Type can be introduced to schools through a formal professional development program presented by a qualified trainer. Those interested may attend and thus an interest in type may be sparked among faculty, staff, and students.

Professional Development

Although there are many strategies for introducing the use of type in schools, we believe the ideal approach is for an entire faculty and staff to participate in a professional development program on type and then agree to work together to apply type in their school. The positive impact on student learning as well as on other aspects of the school, such as the school environment and the relationships among the people in the school, will be considerable when this approach is used.

Professional development is a critical first step to the successful implementation of the use of type in schools. Once type has been introduced, there should be ample opportunities to discuss, practice, and reinforce this knowledge through *ongoing* professional development. Faculty need time to experience and learn about type so that they can create their own continuing education experiences through such activities as the collegial consultation that provides peer critique and suggestions, applications in teamwork situations, and applications of type with students. Teachers also benefit from having resources including books and other materials about type available for their ongoing use.

Advice for the Qualified Trainer

Determine who makes the staff development decisions for the organization you wish to reach, learn what you can about the leader's (principal, superintendent, leadership team chairperson) priorities and main concerns for the academic year, and then use type principles when preparing your proposal. Be prepared to both listen to that person's or committee's goals for the activity (Introversion) as well as explain what you offer and how it fits with the goals (Extraversion). Be prepared with both specific information (Sensing) and a presentation of the big picture (Intuition), with the major points of your presentation (Thinking) as well as the human value to be derived (Feeling), and with a clear plan (Judging) as well as a willingness to adapt as needed (Perceiving). Provide written materials and/or offer to give the Myers-Briggs Type Indicator® instrument and interpret the results for the leader or to the committee as a means of providing an introduction to type.

Following are some benefits of implementing type that you may want to include in the proposal:

- Teachers and staff members increase their self-knowledge—including their areas of strength as well as their challenges.
- Teachers and staff members learn to value work-style differences and learn ways to work together, support each other, and to communicate more effectively.
- Teachers focus on key elements of their own cognitive processes and how they may differ from the students whose minds they are trying to engage.
- Teachers gain insight about how differences in students' learning preferences can determine the degree of effectiveness of their lessons with students.
- Teachers learn specific strategies for personalizing instruction, classroom environment, and assessment that engages different kinds of minds most effectively.
- Teachers learn how to minimize discipline issues with a personalized approach.
- Type is based on valuing differences, and thus type in the school environment enhances the efforts made to welcome and appreciate diversity.

Educators are trained to adhere to recognized standards of instruments and so are likely to ask for information on instrument reliability and validity in addition to details about the research behind the instrument. The MBTI® manual provides this type of information. You can also let educators know that information about type and leadership, and type and teamwork, is also available from various sources. You can share information about the Center for the Application of Psychological Type (CAPT) and point them to the CAPT MBTI bibliography and databank that includes listings of thousands of studies conducted over decades on applications of type. Access is available through the CAPT Web site at www.capt.org. Valuable information is also available at www.aptinternational.org, the Web site of the Association for Psychological Type International.

Administration of the MBTI® Instrument

It is possible to introduce type into the learning process without the use of a formal instrument. However, experience has shown that interest is higher, credibility is more likely, and learning is retained and applied when participants have the opportunity to take an instrument. The MBTI assessment is easy to administer and is not as costly as some instruments; so we recommend its use. There are several options available from the publisher for administration and scoring.

They all require that people purchasing and interpreting the Indicator meet established criteria.

Our personal experience shows that the following two options are optimal when working with school faculty: (1) An online administration arranged through the publisher with the results sent to the qualified trainer to be distributed at the workshop, or (2) use of a self-scorable form administered in the workshop. Either of these methods simplifies the logistics and assures confidentiality of results for the participants.

Following are some important ethical considerations to share with the group when using the MBTI instrument:

- Taking the instrument is voluntary. People can participate in the professional development program on type even if they choose *not to take the instrument*. It is a good idea to have available a few copies of the self-scorable form in case someone who had initially chosen not to take the instrument decides to during the workshop.

- Results are intended for the individual (and the person giving MBTI feedback) and should otherwise remain confidential. Only the individual can verify whether the results are accurate and he or she decides what, if anything, to share with others.

- When presenting to a large group, schedule time to answer questions about individual reports—perhaps over lunch or at the end of the session.

Type Workshop Agenda

Keeping in mind the needs of a variety of types, the agenda for the initial workshop or presentation on type should include these four components:

- Basic information on type
- Opportunity to see type in action
- Opportunity to verify and affirm one's own type
- Applications related to the classroom and school

Completing this agenda generally requires the equivalent of a full day with planned follow-up discussion and activities. The resources included with this book are designed for reproduction and to support your workshop use.

Follow-up

We recommend establishing a partnership with the school or other educational organization where training will be conducted. The partnership can be established between an external consultant or trainer and a designated teacher or administrator who serves as an internal consultant and liaison with the external contractor. It's worth stating again: A one-shot approach has limited effect; teachers and staff need time to experience and learn about type. The outside consultant can serve as a resource as the faculty grows in its knowledge. This consultant or trainer might be an MBTI certified person on the staff or an outside consultant. Regardless, the program will be much more productive and successful when faculty and staff have a specific person to contact to answer questions, address concerns, suggest resources, and provide a general sense of what is or is not working well. Scheduling periodic meetings with department or grade team leaders, as well as a follow up workshop for the entire faculty and staff, increases retention of knowledge and fosters application. When possible, arrange for consultation with groups or individual teachers who want coaching on classroom applications or ways to engage particular students. These provisions should be included in the original contract.

Role of the Principal

The principal is critical to successfully introducing type in a school. Principals can help teachers understand that type differences can profoundly affect student response in the classroom. Principals can recognize teachers who incorporate knowledge about type differences in the design of their lessons and adjust their teaching based on these differences. The principal can encourage teachers to draw on the expertise that exists among their colleagues. Principals can encourage people to work together in collaborative teams. They can provide training for teachers, create the conditions for learning, and share strategies to address the individual needs of students.

The principal can provide support, encouragement, and opportunities for the faculty to increase their understanding and applications of type knowledge. This support can begin with the principal sharing his or her own type and its implications for an effective working relationship with the faculty. Time at faculty meetings can be used for activities that help teachers experience type at work. For example, teachers of the same type can meet as a group, describe their own positive learning experiences, and share these in written or oral form with other groups of teachers. (See Resource 4, *Learning with the Preferences*.)

One very effective principal used part of each faculty meeting to showcase what an individual teacher was doing to engage the different kinds of minds present in that teacher's classroom. This activity was made even more valuable because the physical facilities made it possible for faculty meetings to be held in the featured classroom.

As instructional leader, the principal can work together with teachers to determine what factors, strategies, and classroom conditions must be in place for student engagement to occur. Resource 6, *Engaging Students of All Types* provides questions principals and teachers can use together as lessons are designed and observed. In addition, other resources (see for instance Resources 1, 2, 5, 9, and 10) contain information on learning and classroom management based on how students of different types learn and perform at their best.

Teacher Colleagues as Consultants

It is important to remember that there is a wealth of knowledge about type already present in schools. Teachers can be encouraged to consult with each other as "experts" on their particular type. Serving as consultants to each other, teachers of different types can share how they best learn in order to help incorporate type into lesson design and student assessment. Teachers do not have to have taught the particular lesson or topic being considered. Deciding how they would like to study the topic or learn the lesson if they were the student works quite well. If a teacher of a different type has already taught the particular lesson in question, he or she can share how they taught it. There is a good chance that his or her teaching method will reflect their type.

GREAT MINDS

"The barriers are not erected which can say to aspiring talents and industry, 'Thus far and no farther.'"

LUDWIG VAN BEETHOVEN (1770–1827) This German composer led the transformation from the classical to the romantic style of music including his transcendent Symphony no. 9, the Choral Symphony, which was composed after he had gone deaf.

Some schools have chosen to organize the process of sharing information about type differences and to meet in small groups on a regular basis for lesson planning. Resource 3, *Teaching with the Preferences*, and Resource 4, *Learning with the Preferences*, are exercises that can be conducted with an entire faculty or a group of teachers in order to understand and practice this consultation process. Some schools have offered continuing education credits to teachers who develop lessons and assessments based on type differences and display or demonstrate these for their colleagues.

Communicating Preferences

Teachers and staff who work together collaboratively can participate in brief discussions, activities, and exercises about topics such as communication styles and preferred ways to be recognized and appreciated. Some examples of helpful questions to be discussed include the following:

- How do I prefer people to communicate with me?
- What motivates me? What "de-motivates" me?
- What approach works best when someone is trying to get me to take on a project or responsibility?
- If I am working on a project, for what and when do I want to be recognized for my work?

Discussing questions like these in the context of type preferences fosters a neutral, more candid discussion that respects and honors individual differences. People who are able to be open and honest in communicating their preferences increase their knowledge of normal human differences and ways to use these differences for the greater good of all their students as well as for their own well-being and working relationships. (Resource 29, *Recognition and Appreciation by Type*, is an exercise which can be used to develop understanding about the preferred ways individuals like to be recognized and appreciated.)

First Things First: Value Your Own Type!

People who are just beginning to learn about type should initially focus on self-awareness. By first building an understanding of how type preferences influence your own life, you can understand your own behaviors and reactions to others. Look for opportunities to observe others of the same type to affirm the natural strengths and learn to recognize potential blind spots that are likely your own as well.

As a teacher, become aware of how you express your type in your lessons, in teaching, in the appearance and climate of your classroom, in the ways you assess learning, and in your approach to students and colleagues. Try some type-based activities in the classroom individually or with colleagues. Assess the outcomes and make adjustments. As principal, become aware of how you express your type in your leadership, your management of school operations, your communications, your recognition of faculty and staff accomplishments, and in your approach to your administrative team, teachers, students, and parents. Try some type-based communication with other people in the school community whose type you gauge to be different from yours. Assess the outcomes and make adjustments.

Observe students through the lens of type and notice how their preferences affect their learning. Continue the process of getting to know others of similar and different types and notice how type influences and helps us understand behavior. Continue to learn about type and share with others what you learn and experience. Through this process of ongoing learning, we are confident you will find that type knowledge has many benefits to your personal life, the lives of students, and life in schools.

To Wrap It Up

Introducing type in schools, while presenting new challenges as people learn new ways to work with and support those of different types and preferences, offers the rewards of greater personal satisfaction, opportunities for learning and collaboration, and increased student achievement. It's not a bad investment!

In a Nutshell

- The ideal approach to introducing type into schools is a total school approach.
- A one-time approach is not effective; teachers need time to experience and learn about type.
- The principal plays an important role in introducing type into a school and provides support, encouragement, and opportunities for the faculty to increase their understanding and application of type knowledge.
- Providing people with the opportunity to take the MBTI instrument may increase the likelihood they will retain the information they learn about type.

Q *What is one possibility for introducing type in schools?*

A Determine who makes the staff development decisions for the school and offer a proposal to conduct a staff development session based on type and learning.

Q *If the MBTI instrument is used, what are important ethical issues to be considered?*

A The taking of the instrument should be voluntary; results should remain confidential, participants need the opportunity to verify their results, and the individual should determine whether or not to share the results with others.

Q *Who are possible consultants teachers can use to increase their knowledge and use of type?*

A Teachers at a school can consult with colleagues, the principal, or a qualified MBTI trainer.

Q *Name two ways principals can support the use of type in schools.*

A (1) Principals can support teachers who incorporate knowledge about type differences in their teaching.

(2) Principals can share their own type and encourage teachers to share their own type and how their type affects their communication style.

CHAPTER 10

Introducing Type

in Schools

Getting Started

- Notice how type affects your behavior.
- Consult with someone who is the same type you are, and share information about your type.
- Discuss how you learn best and the implications for student learning.
- Try some type-based activities with students in the classroom, assess the outcomes, and make adjustments.

Teachers, Elementary School
N = 1030

The Sixteen Complete Types			
ISTJ	**ISFJ**	**INFJ**	**INTJ**
N = 92	N = 123	N = 52	N = 22
% = 8.93	% = 11.94	% = 5.05	% = 2.14
■■■■■■■■	■■■■■■■■■■■■ ■	■■■■■	■■
ISTP	**ISFP**	**INFP**	**INTP**
N = 23	N = 37	N = 64	N = 22
% = 2.23	% = 3.59	% = 6.21	% = 2.14
■■	■■■	■■■■■■	■■
ESTP	**ESFP**	**ENFP**	**ENTP**
N = 18	N = 59	N = 147	N = 29
% = 1.75	% = 5.73	% = 14.27	% = 2.82
■	■■■■■	■■■■■■■■■■■ ■■■■	
ESTJ	**ESFJ**	**ENFJ**	**ENTJ**
N = 66	N = 151	N = 94	N = 31
% = 6.41	% = 14.66	% = 9.13	% = 3.01
■■■■■■	■■■■■■■■■■■■ ■■■■■■■■ ■■■■	■■■	

Note: ■ = 1 percent

Dichotomous Preferences	N	%
E	595	57.77
I	435	42.23
S	569	55.24
N	461	44.76
T	303	29.42
F	727	70.58
J	631	61.26
P	399	38.74

Pairs and Temperaments	N	%
I J	289	28.06
I P	146	14.17
E P	253	24.56
E J	342	33.20
S T	199	19.32
S F	370	35.92
N F	357	34.66
N T	104	10.10
S J	432	41.94
S P	137	13.30
N P	262	25.44
N J	199	19.32
T J	211	20.49
T P	92	8.93
F P	307	29.81
F J	420	40.78
I N	160	15.53
E N	301	29.22
I S	275	26.70
E S	294	28.54
E T	144	13.98
E F	451	43.79
I F	276	26.80
I T	159	15.44

Jungian Types (E)	N	%
E - T J	97	9.42
E - F J	245	23.79
E S - P	77	7.48
E N - P	176	17.09

Jungian Types (I)	N	%
I - T P	45	4.37
I - F P	101	9.81
I S - J	215	20.87
I N - J	74	7.18

Dominant Types	N	%
Dt. T	142	13.79
Dt. F	346	33.59
Dt. S	292	28.35
Dt. N	250	24.27

Source: CPP Data Base, Elementary School Teachers (N=1030). 118 male, 910 female, average age 37. Published in Schaubhut, N. A., & Thompson, R. C. (2008). MBTI Type Tables for Occupations. Mountain View, CA: CPP, Inc.

APPENDIX

Teachers, Middle School
N = 652

The Sixteen Complete Types

ISTJ	ISFJ	INFJ	INTJ
N = 61	N = 56	N = 40	N = 16
% = 9.36	% = 8.59	% = 6.13	% = 2.45
■■■■■■■■■	■■■■■■■■	■■■■■■	■■

ISTP	ISFP	INFP	INTP
N = 12	N = 19	N = 45	N = 22
% = 1.84	% = 2.91	% = 6.90	% = 3.37
■	■■	■■■■■■	■■■

ESTP	ESFP	ENFP	ENTP
N = 30	N = 42	N = 85	N = 37
% = 4.60	% = 6.44	% = 13.04	% = 5.67
■■■■	■■■■■■	■■■■■■■■■■■■■ ■■■■■ ■■■	■■■

ESTJ	ESFJ	ENFJ	ENTJ
N = 61	N = 50	N = 41	N = 35
% = 9.36	% = 7.67	% = 6.29	% = 5.37
■■■■■■■■■	■■■■■■■	■■■■■■	■■■■■

Note: ■ = 1 percent

Dichotomous Preferences

	N	%
E	381	58.44
I	271	41.56
S	331	50.77
N	321	49.23
T	274	42.02
F	378	57.98
J	360	55.21
P	292	44.79

Pairs and Temperaments

	N	%
I J	173	26.53
I P	98	15.03
E P	194	29.75
E J	187	28.68
ST	164	25.15
SF	167	25.61
NF	211	32.36
NT	110	16.87
SJ	228	34.97
SP	103	15.80
NP	189	28.99
NJ	132	20.25
TJ	173	26.53
TP	101	15.49
FP	191	29.29
FJ	187	28.68
I N	123	18.87
EN	198	30.37
I S	148	22.70
ES	183	28.07
ET	163	25.00
EF	218	33.44
I F	160	24.54
I T	111	17.02

Jungian Types (E)

	N	%
E - T J	96	14.72
E - F J	91	13.96
ES - P	72	11.04
EN - P	122	18.71

Jungian Types (I)

	N	%
I - TP	34	5.21
I - FP	64	9.82
IS - J	117	17.94
IN - J	56	8.59

Dominant Types

	N	%
Dt. T	130	19.94
Dt. F	155	23.77
Dt. S	189	28.99
Dt. N	178	27.30

Source: CPP Data Base, Middle School Teachers (N=652). 192 male, 460 female, average age 37. Published in Schaubhut, N. A., & Thompson, R. C. (2008). MBTI Type Tables for Occupations. Mountain View, CA: CPP, Inc.

Teachers, Secondary School
N = 889

The Sixteen Complete Types

ISTJ	ISFJ	INFJ	INTJ
N = 102	N = 60	N = 36	N = 48
% = 11.47	% = 6.75	% = 4.05	% = 5.40

ISTP	ISFP	INFP	INTP
N = 36	N = 17	N = 67	N = 44
% = 4.05	% = 1.91	% = 7.54	% = 4.95

ESTP	ESFP	ENFP	ENTP
N = 25	N = 35	N = 103	N = 58
% = 2.81	% = 3.94	% = 11.59	% = 6.52

ESTJ	ESFJ	ENFJ	ENTJ
N = 90	N = 66	N = 66	N = 36
% = 10.12	% = 7.42	% = 7.42	% = 4.05

Note: ■ = 1 percent

Dichotomous Preferences

	N	%
E	479	53.88
I	410	46.12
S	431	48.48
N	458	51.52
T	439	49.38
F	450	50.62
J	504	56.69
P	385	43.31

Pairs and Temperaments

	N	%
I J	246	27.67
I P	164	18.45
E P	221	24.86
E J	258	29.02
ST	253	28.46
SF	178	20.02
NF	272	30.60
NT	186	20.92
SJ	318	35.77
SP	113	12.71
NP	272	30.60
NJ	186	20.92
TJ	276	31.05
TP	163	18.34
FP	222	24.97
FJ	228	25.65
I N	195	21.93
EN	263	29.58
I S	215	24.18
ES	216	24.30
ET	209	23.51
EF	270	30.37
I F	180	20.25
I T	230	25.87

Jungian Types (E)

	N	%
E - TJ	126	14.17
E - FJ	132	14.85
ES - P	60	6.75
EN - P	161	18.11

Jungian Types (I)

	N	%
I - TP	80	9.00
I - FP	84	9.45
IS - J	162	18.22
IN - J	84	9.45

Dominant Types

	N	%
Dt. T	206	23.17
Dt. F	216	24.30
Dt. S	222	24.97
Dt. N	245	27.56

Source: CPP Data Base, Secondary School Teachers (N=889). 370 male, 517 female, average age 37. Published in Schaubhut, N. A., & Thompson, R. C. (2008). MBTI Type Tables for Occupations. Mountain View, CA: CPP, Inc.

APPENDIX

USA: Distribution of the Types in the National Representative Sample

(Total = 3,009, Males = 1,478, Females = 1,531)

ISTJ	ISFJ	INFJ	INTJ
T = 11.6%	T = 13.8%	T = 1.5%	T = 2.1%
M = 16.4%	M = 8.1%	M = 1.2%	M = 3.3%
F = 6.9%	F = 19.4%	F = 1.6%	F = 0.9%
ISTP	**ISFP**	**INFP**	**INTP**
T = 5.4%	T = 8.8%	T = 4.4%	T = 3.3%
M = 8.5%	M = 7.6%	M = 4.1%	M = 4.8%
F = 2.3%	F = 9.9%	F = 4.6%	F = 1.7%
ESTP	**ESFP**	**ENFP**	**ENTP**
T = 4.3%	T = 8.5%	T = 8.1%	T = 3.2%
M = 5.6%	M = 6.9%	M = 6.4%	M = 4.0%
F = 3.0%	F = 10.1%	F = 9.7%	F = 2.4%
ESTJ	**ESFJ**	**ENFJ**	**ENTJ**
T = 8.7%	T = 12.3%	T = 2.5%	T = 1.8%
M = 11.2%	M = 7.5%	M = 1.6%	M = 2.7%
F = 6.3%	F = 16.9%	F = 3.3%	F = 0.9%

ISTJ	ISFJ	INFJ	INTJ
T = 348	T = 416	T = 44	T = 62
M = 242	M = 119	M = 19	M = 49
F = 106	F = 297	F = 25	F = 13
ISTP	**ISFP**	**INFP**	**INTP**
T = 162	T = 264	T = 132	T = 98
M = 126	M = 112	M = 61	M = 71
F = 36	F = 152	F = 71	F = 27
ESTP	**ESFP**	**ENFP**	**ENTP**
T = 129	T = 256	T = 243	T = 96
M = 83	M = 102	M = 95	M = 59
F = 46	F = 154	F = 148	F = 37
ESTJ	**ESFJ**	**ENFJ**	**ENTJ**
T = 261	T = 370	T = 74	T = 54
M = 165	M = 111	M = 24	M = 40
F = 96	F = 259	F = 50	F = 14

Total	Males	Females
E 49.3%, I 50.7%	E 45.9%, I 54.1%	E 52.5%, I 47.5%
S 73.3%, N 26.7%	S 71.7%, N 28.3%	S 74.9%, N 25.1%
T 40.2%, F 59.8%	T 56.5%, F 43.5%	T 24.5%, F 75.5%
J 54.1%, P 45.9%	J 52.0%, P 48.0%	J 56.2%, P 43.8%

SOURCE: Myers, I.B., McCaulley, M. H., Quenk, N. L., & Hammer, A. L. (1998). *MBTI® Manual: A guide to the development and use of the Myers-Briggs Type Indicator* (3rd ed.). Palo Alto, CA: CPP, Inc. (Males, pg. 15; Females, p. 158; Totals, p. 298; Races, p. 156, 379; Demographics, pp. 385–386)

Chapter 1

1. Conversation with the author, 1989.

2. As reported to the authors by Mary McCaulley, Ph.D., Isabel Myers' colleague and founder of the Center for Applications of Psychological Type, personal conversation, 1987.

Chapter 2

1. Sharon Fitzsimmons, *Type and Time Management* (Edmonton: Psychometrics Canada Ltd., 1999).

2. For additional groupings commonly and effectively used, see Resource 2 and 7. Lesson examples are provided for each of these groupings as well as the function-pair grouping we use in this book.

3. Henry Michael Seiden, "Time Perspective and Styles of Consciousness: An Exploratory Study" (Ph.D. diss., New School for Social Research), abstract in *Dissertation Abstracts International* 31 (1969): 31–01B.

4. Conversation with author, 1996.

5. Nina L. Lepes, "Time Estimation and Individual Differences in Junior High School Students." (Ph.D. diss., Fordham University), abstract in *Dissertation Abstracts International* 43 (1983):12A.

6. "Joy in Closure" to describe the Judging attitude and "Joy in Process" to describe the Perceiving attitude were first suggested by the late Susan Brock, Ph.D.

Chapter 3

1. *Breaking Ranks II: Strategies for Leading High School Reform.* Reston, VA: National Association of Secondary School Principals, 2004, 69.

2. David A. Sousa, *How the Brain Learns* (Reston, VA: National Association of Secondary School Principals, 1995), 20.

3. Leverne Barrett, "Impact of Teacher Personality on Classroom Environment," *Journal of Psychological Type* 18 (1989):56.

Chapter 4

1. Rieneke Zessoules and Howard Gardner, "Authentic Assessment Beyond the Buzzword and into the Classroom." In V. Perrone (Ed.), *Expanding Student Assessment* (Alexandria, VA: Association for Supervision and Curriculum Development, 1991), 54.

2. Mary H. McCaulley, letter to authors, August 30, 1993.

3. Isabel Briggs Myers et al., *MBTI Manual: A Guide to the Development and Use of the Myers-Briggs Type Indicator*®, 3rd ed. (Palo Alto: Consulting Psychologists Press, Inc., 1998), 267.

4. Reported by S and N groups in many workshops conducted by Sondra VanSant.

5. Isabel Briggs Myers, *Gifts Differing* (Palo Alto: Consulting Psychologists Press, Inc., 1980), 152.

6. Ibid.

7. Marti Maguire, "Mind-bending SAT No Longer Stands Alone," *News & Observer* (Raleigh, NC), 4 January 2006, final edition.

8. Myers, et al., *MBTI Manual*, 269.

9. Jay McTighe and Ken O'Connor, "Seven Practices for Effective Learning," *Educational Leadership* 63 (2005): 15.

Chapter 5

1. Gordon Lawrence, "Sharing New Assumptions to Guide Education in the New Century" (paper presented at symposium, "Orchestrating Educational Change in the 90s: The Role of Psychological Type," Center for Applications of Psychological Type, Gainesville, FL, 1994).

2. C. G. Jung, *Psychological Types*, revision of R.F.C. Hull of the translation by H.G. Baynes. (Princeton University Press, 1971), 450.

3. For more information on development of type in adulthood, readers may be interested in *Introduction to Type Dynamics and Development* by Katharine Myers and Linda Kirby (Mountain View, CA: CPP, Inc., 1994); *Was that Really Me? How Everyday Stress Brings Out Our Hidden Personality* by Naomi Quenk (Mountain View, CA: CPP, Inc. 2002); and *Jung's Typology* by Marie-Louise von Franz and James Hillman (Dallas: Spring Publications, Inc., 1971).

4. Howard Gardner, *Intelligence Reframed: Multiple Intelligences for the 21st Century* (New York: Basic Books, 1991).

5. Isabel Myers, *Gifts Differing* (Mountain View, CA: CPP, Inc., 1980).

6. Ibid., 150.

7. See Myers and McCaulley, 1985 *MBTI Manual*; Myers, et al., 3rd ed. *MBTI Manual* 1998; Hammer, Ed., *MBTI Applications*, CAPT bibliography available at www.capt.org for listing.

8. Myers, *Gifts Differing*, 1980.

Chapter 6

1. *Breaking Ranks II: Strategies for Leading High School Reform*. xi. Reston, VA. National Association of Secondary School Principals, 2004, xi.

Chapter 7

1. Gordon Lawrence, *People Types and Tiger Stripes*, 3rd ed. (Gainesville, FL: CAPT, 1993), 161.
2. Donald Lueder, "The Trait Theory Revisited: Principals' Personalities and Perceived Leadership Behavior," *National Forum of Educational Administration and Supervision* 2 (1983):58–67.

Chapter 8

1. Kenneth Thomas, *Introduction to Conflict Management* (Mountain View, CA: CPP, Inc., 2002).
2. Terrance Q. Percival, Verner Smitheram, and Margaret Kelly, "Myers-Briggs Type Indicator and Conflict-Handling Intention: An Interactive Approach," *Journal of Psychological Type* 23 (1992): 10–16.
3. Alan K. Johnson, "Conflict-Handling Intentions and the MBTI: A Construct Validity," *Journal of Psychological Type* 43 (1997): 29–39.
4. For a more comprehensive discussion and examples of using type to resolve or manage conflict, see Sondra VanSant, *Wired for Conflict: The Role of Personality in Resolving Differences* (Gainesville, FL: CAPT, 2003).

Chapter 9

1. VanSant, *Wired for Conflict*, 13.
2. Ibid., 22.
3. Ibid., 18.

Bibliography

Barr, Lee and Norma Barr. *The Leadership Equation.* Austin, TX: Eakin Press, 1989.

Barrett, Leverne. "Impact of Teacher Personality on Classroom Environment." *Journal of Psychological Type* 18 (1989): 50–56.

Blankstein, Alan M. *Failure Is Not an Option.* Thousand Oaks, CA: Corwin Press, 2004.

Breaking Ranks II™: Strategies for Leading High School Reform. Reston, VA: National Association of Secondary School Principals, 2004.

Brownsword, Alan W. *Psychological Type: An Introduction.* San Anselmo: The Human Resources Management Press, Inc., 1988.

——. *The Type Descriptions.* San Anselmo: The Human Resources Management Press, Inc., 1990.

DuFour, Richard and Robert Eaker. *Professional Communities at Work: Best Practices for Enhancing Student Achievement.* Bloomington, IN: Solution Tree Press, 1998.

Eaker, Robert; Richard DuFour; and Rebecca Burnette. *Getting Started: Reculturing Schools to Become Professional Learning Communities.* Bloomington, IN: Solution Tree Press, 2002.

Fairhurst, Alice M. and Lisa L. Fairhurst. *Effective Teaching, Effective Learning: Making the Personality Connection in Your Classroom.* Mountain View, CA: CPP, Inc., 1995.

Fisher, Roger and William Ury. *Getting to Yes: Negotiating Agreement Without Giving In.* New York: Penguin Books, 1991.

Fitzsimmons, Sharon. *Type and Time Management.* Edmonton: Psychometrics Canada Ltd., 1999.

Fullan, Michael. *The Moral Imperative of School Leadership.* Thousand Oaks, CA: Corwin Press, 2003.

Gardner, Howard. *Intelligence Reframed: Multiple Intelligences for the 21st Century.* New York: Basic Books, 1999.

Golay, Keith. *Learning Patterns and Temperament Styles.* Fullerton, CA: MANAS-SYSTEMS, 1982.

Hammer, Allen L., ed. *MBTI Applications: A Decade of Research on the Myers-Briggs Type Indicator®.* Mountain View, CA: CPP, Inc., 1993.

Hirsh, Sandra Krebs, and Jane A. G. Kise. *Using the MBTI Tool in Organizations.* 3rd ed. Mountain View, CA: CPP, Inc.v, 2001.

——. *Introduction to Type and Coaching.* Mountain View, CA: CPP, Inc., 2000.

Johnson, Alan K. "Conflict-Handling Intentions and the MBTI: A Construct Validity." *Journal of Psychological Type* 43 (1997): 29–39.

Jung, Carl G. *Psychological Types.* Revision by R.F.C. Hull of the translation by H.G. Baynes. Princeton University Press, 1971.

Keirsey, David and Marilyn Bates. *Please Understand Me.* Del Mar, CA: Prometheus Nemesis Book Company, 1978.

Keirsey, David. *Please Understand Me II,* Del Mar, CA: Prometheus Nemesis Book Company, 1998.

Kise, J. A. G. *Differentiated coaching: A framework for helping teachers change.* Thousand Oaks, CA: Corwin Press, 2006.

Kise, J. A. G. *Differentiation through personality types: A framework for instruction, assessment, and classroom management.* Thousand Oaks, CA: Corwin Press, 2007.

Kise, J. A. G., & Russell, B. *Differentiated school leadership: Effective collaboration, communication, and change through personality type.* Thousand Oaks, CA: Corwin Press, 2008.

Knowles, Malcom S.; Elwood F. Holton; and Richard A. Swansson. *The Adult Learner,* rev. ed. Burlington, MA: Elsevier, 2005.

Lawrence, Gordon. *People Types and Tiger Stripes.* 3rd ed. Gainesville, FL: CAPT, 1993.

——. *Descriptions of the Sixteen Types.* Gainesville, FL: CAPT, 1995.

——. "Sharing New Assumptions to Guide Education in the New Century." Paper presented at Symposium. "Orchestrating Educational Change in the 90s: The Role of Psychological Type." Gainesville, FL: CAPT, 1994.

Lepes, Nina L. "Time Estimation and Individual Differences in Junior High School Students." Ph.D. diss., Fordham University, 1983. Abstract in *Dissertation Abstracts International* 43(12): 3894A.

Levine, Mel. *A Mind at a Time.* New York: Simon & Schuster, 2002.

Lueder, Donald. "The Trait Theory Revisited: Principals' Personalities and Perceived Leadership Behavior." *National Forum of Educational Administration and Supervision* 2 (1983): 58–67.

McTighe, Jay and Ken O'Connor. "Seven Practices for Effective Learning." *Educational Leadership* 63 (2005): 10–17.

McCaulley, Mary. *The Myers-Briggs Type Indicator and Leadership.* Gainesville, FL: CAPT, 1990.

Maguire, Marti. "Mind-bending SAT No Longer Stands Alone." *Raleigh News & Observer.* 4 January 2006.

Marzano, Robert. *What Works in Schools: Translating Research into Action.* Alexandria, VA: Association for Supervision and Curriculum Development, 2003.

Marzano, Robert J., Debra J. Pickering, and Jane E. Pollock. *Classroom Instruction that Works.* Alexandria, VA: Association for Supervision and Curriculum Development, 2001.

Meisgeier, Charles; Elizabeth Murphy; and Constance Meisgeier. *A Teacher's Guide to Type: A New Perspective on Individual Differences in the Classroom.* Mountain View, CA: CPP, Inc., 1989.

Myers, Isabel Briggs with Peter B. Myers. *Gifts Differing.* Palo Alto: Mountain View, CA: CPP, Inc., 1980.

Myers, Isabel Briggs. *Type and Teamwork.* Gainesville, FL: CAPT, 1974.

Myers, Isabel Briggs, Mary H. McCaulley, Naomi L. Quenk, and Allan L. Hammer. *MBTI Manual: A Guide to the Development and Use of the Myers-Briggs Type Indicator®*, 3rd ed. Mountain View, CA: CPP, Inc., 1998.

Myers, Katharine and Linda Kirby. *Introduction to Type Dynamics and Development.* Mountain View, CA: CPP, Inc., 1994.

Percival, Terrance Q.; Verner Smitheram; and Margaret Kelly. "Myers-Briggs Type Indicator and Conflict-Handling Intention: An Interactive Approach." *Journal of Psychological Type* 23 (1992): 10–16.

Provost, Judith A. *Strategies for Success: Using Type to Do Better in High School and College.* Gainesville, FL: CAPT, 1992.

Quenk, Naomi. *Beside Ourselves.* Mountain View, CA: CPP, Inc.,1993.

Seiden, Henry Michael. "Time Perspective and Styles of Consciousness: An Exploratory Study." Ph.D. Diss., New School for Social Research, 1969. Abstract in *Dissertation Abstracts International* 31(1969):31–01B.

Sousa, David A. *How the Brain Learns.* Reston, VA: National Association of Secondary School Principals, 1995.

Sweet, Janie D. "A Method of Assessing Jungian Psychological Type Development in a High School Student Sample." Ph.D. diss., University of Florida, 1982. Abstract in *Dissertation Abstracts International* 31(01): 386B.

Thomas, Kenneth. *Introduction to Conflict Management.* Mountain View, CA: CPP, Inc., 2002.

Zessoules, R. and H. Gardner. "Authentic Assessment Beyond the Buzzword and into the Classroom." In V. Perrone (Ed.), *Expanding Student Assessment* (p.54) Alexandria, VA: Association for Supervision and Curriculum Development, 1991.

VanSant, Sondra. *Wired for Conflict: The Role of Personality in Resolving Differences.* Gainesville, FL: CAPT, 2003.

Von Franz, Marie-Louise and James Hillman. *Jung's Typology.* Dallas: Spring Publications Inc., 1971.

About the Authors

Diane Payne has been a teacher, counselor, university administrator, and high school principal for more than twenty years. Diane is currently an associate with the Leadership Group of the Carolinas where she serves as a leadership facilitator to high schools in North Carolina. In addition to being a principal, Diane has served as a faculty member of the Principals' Executive Program at the University of North Carolina at Chapel Hill and as a member of several committees of the National Association of Secondary School Principals including the High School Task Force and the National Alliance of High Schools Advisory Council. Diane has published articles in *The High School Magazine*, the *NASSP Bulletin*, and *Principal Leadership* and written a handbook on *Identifying Effective Teaching in the Classroom*. She coauthored with Sondra VanSant *Psychological Type in Schools: Applications for Educators*. She was the MetLife/NASSP Principal of the Year for North Carolina (2000) and recognized as a Distinguished Alumnus of the School of Education of the University of North Carolina in Chapel Hill. In 2005, Diane received the Order of the Long Leaf Pine for distinguished service to North Carolina.

Diane lives in Raleigh, North Carolina, with her husband Mike and has two daughters and three grandchildren.

Sondra VanSant has more than 30 years experience as a counselor, teacher, trainer, and consultant. She maintained a private practice in Chapel Hill, North Carolina, for many years and has worked as a counselor and teacher in public and private schools. She is a faculty member of the Principals' Executive Program at the University of North Carolina and has worked with many school systems and faculties to help them work together effectively in teams, to understand how students learn differently, and to design curriculum and instruction to accommodate these differences. She is coauthor with Diane Payne of the first edition of this book, entitled *Psychological Type in Schools: Applications for Educators*. She is also author of *Wired for Conflict: The Role of Personality in Resolving Differences*, also published by CAPT, and a number of articles. Her seminar and workshop leadership has also involved private corporations large and small and federal and state government agencies, covering topics related to leadership, conflict management, group dynamics, and career development. She served as a faculty member of the Association for Psychological Type's MBTI® Qualifying Program, as a career counselor for the USA Today online edition, and frequently speaks at conferences.

Sondra lives in Chapel Hill with her husband, Jerry, and their "surrogate grandchild," labradoodle Meg. Their two children live nearby.

Introduction to Resources

The following list provides a comprehensive inventory of reproducible exercises and handouts for use by teachers and administrators, as well as by coaches and trainers of educators. They are saved in a print-friendly, pdf format on the CD-ROM located on the inside back cover of this book. They are designed as application supplements to the chapters in this handbook. Supporting information for each resource can be found in the related handbook chapters.

Resource 1, *Type Preferences and Learning: A Quick Reference Guide,* provides a chart with a general description of the impact of each preference on learning. It can be used as a quick reference guide.

Resource 2, *Learning Preferences by Type: Words and Activities that Work,* provides a reference list of ways students of different types approach a learning task and are engaged or become disengaged by the specific words and activities utilized. Teachers will find this list helpful as they design lessons to reach all students.

Resource 3, *Teaching with the Preferences,* is an exercise which demonstrates experientially the relevance of type to teaching and learning and enables teachers to experience these differences with their peers. Participants work in groups in developing and demonstrating a brief introduction to a lesson.

Resource 4, *Learning with the Preferences,* is another exercise which demonstrates the relevance of type to teaching and learning. Participants in type-alike groups describe how they best learn, demonstrate their knowledge, and become involved in a learning community.

Resource 5, *Make Good Lessons Even More Engaging,* includes two versions of an exercise to help teachers gain skill in modifying and personalizing lessons to engage all types in the classroom. One version is designed for type-diverse groupings, the other for type-alike groupings.

Resource 6, *Engaging Students of all Types*, includes two handouts. The first handout can be used as a guide for teachers in evaluating how likely they are to engage each of the eight preferences of type in a particular lesson or sometime during a particular day. The second handout provides a template that teachers can use to organize the content of lessons already developed to explore additional strategies to engage all the types.

Resource 7, *Sample Lessons Incorporating Type*, is a collection of sample lessons teachers can review as examples of offering students choices for how they accomplish a particular competency. Examples are given for elementary, middle and high schools. Some examples are based on the Funtional Pairs, others on Quadrants, the four Mental Functions, or Temperament groupings of type preferences.

Resource 8, *Type and Time*, provides information about ways different personality types use time. The handout is useful for understanding students' work styles and helping them learn to manage their time.

Resource 9, *Type and Work Space*, provides a summary of information compiled from different types describing their preferences for ideal working space. The resource can serve as a guide for arranging space and furniture to accommodate different needs to the extent possible.

Resource 10, *Preventing Discipline Problems*, provides information to help teachers develop strategies based on type preferences to prevent or correct student discipline problems. The handout can be used to help teachers identify possible type-based sources for discipline problems and strategies that can be used both for intervention and prevention.

Resource 11, *How Would You Intervene?* is an exercise to help teachers build skills in exploring type-based interventions for students who are not fully engaged in the classroom. The case studies can be used for teachers to develop skills to engage students who are struggling in school and seem disconnected with the learning process.

Resource 12, *Developing Assessment Criteria: A Guide for Teachers,* shows how teachers can apply the use of all four functions of Sensing, Intuition, Thinking, and Feeling to the process of developing assessments.

Resource 13, *Test Questions: Differences for Sensing and Intuition*, shows how teachers can word test-questions to accommodate the Sensing and Intuition differences of their students. The resource provides a wording of test questions that are more likely to engage students with a preference for Sensing and students with a preference for Intuition.

Resource 14, *Student Self-Assessment*, includes a series of handouts for teachers to help students learn to self-assess their work.

Resource 15, *Helping Students Develop Their Preferences: Teacher Tips*, provides techniques teachers can use for engaging students' natural preferences and helps teachers make certain they accommodate the different preferences of their students.

Resource 16, *Mind Mapping and Mind Structuring*, provides two exercises: one for developing Intuition through a flow of ideas and one for developing Sensing by structuring specific information which supports an idea.

Resource 17, *To Do My Best Work I Need . . .* provides information for teachers to help them understand the specific needs of each of their students and provides students an opportunity to give information about what they need from the teacher and themselves in order to do their best work.

Resource 18, *Team Analysis*, is an exercise for teams to analyze individual members' strengths and potential weaknesses, determine team effectiveness, and discuss ways to enhance the ability to function effectively as a team.

Resource 19, *Type Tables*, includes a reproducible, blank type table which can be used as a visual for the distribution of types in a particular group and a type table which indicates the order of preferences for each of the 16 types.

Resource 20, *Research Summary: Principals' Problem-Solving Strategies*, provides the results of a study on problem solving strategies used by school principals.

Resource 21, *Case Study for Problem Solving Using the Z Model*, is an exercise which illustrates how the Z model of problem solving can be used and provides an opportunity for participants to see how knowledge of type enhances understanding of different views of a situation.

Resource 22, *Type Specific Tips for Problem Solving*, provides suggestions to use when problem solving according to people's preferences for Extraversion, Introversion, Sensing, Intuition, Thinking, Feeling, Judging, and Perceiving.

Resource 23, *Type Preferences and Conflict: A Quick Reference Guide*, provides basic information on type and conflict across all eight preferences.

Resource 24, *Conflict and Type*, is a summary of the actual data collected by the authors from the types in numerous workshops on conflict showing differing definitions and views of conflict, typical sources of conflict, characteristics of good resolutions, and reactions and approaches to resolving conflict.

Resource 25, *Type Differences in Conflict*, is an exercise to demonstrate and compare similarities and differences in definitions of and reactions to conflict, and to learn strategies to resolve conflicts based on an understanding of type differences. The exercise produces results from the participants in a workshop or conflict management session and is a process which can be used to obtain the information provided in Resource 24.

Resource 26, *Case Study for Resolving Conflict*, is an exercise designed to reveal different ways of problem solving and provides an opportunity for participants to see how knowledge of type enhances understanding of different views of a situation. The case study exercise based on a teacher-teacher conflict is designed to demonstrate differences in Thinking and Feeling responses to conflict.

Resource 27, *Teacher-Student Conflict: The Hat in Class*, is an exercise which can be used to assist with the understanding of type differences in resolving conflict using a simulated encounter between a principal and teacher of different types attempting to resolve a teacher-student conflict.

Resource 28, *Nonverbal Type Differences in Conflict*, is an exercise to demonstrate the significant differences a person's preferences for Extraversion or Introversion and Judging or Perceiving make on nonverbal behaviors in conflict resolution.

Resource 29, *Recognition and Appreciation by Type*, is an exercise which allows individual team members to describe their preferences for the type of performance recognition they prefer and how they would like appreciation to be shown to them.

Ethical Guidelines for Using the
Myers-Briggs Type Indicator® Instrument

- Identify type theory as the work of C.G. Jung and the instrument as the work of Isabel Briggs Myers and Katharine C. Briggs.

- Present psychological type as describing healthy personality differences, not psychological disorders or fixed traits.

- Be adamant that all types are valuable: no type is better, healthier, or more desirable in any way.

- Describe preference and types in nonjudgmental terms at all times; be aware of how your own type biases may influence your words.

- Present type preferences as tendencies, preferences, or inclinations, rather than absolutes.

- Stress that type does not imply excellence, competence, or natural ability, only what is preferred.

- Never imply that all people of a certain type behave in the same way; type should not encourage stereotyping or be used to put people in rigid categories.

- Explain how people sometimes act in ways contrary to their preferences because of pressure from family, relationships, job environment, or culture. Consistent forced use of non preferences can cause stress.

- When describing preferences, distinguish between what has been shown by research and what are anecdotes to illustrate type.

- Provide appropriate interpretation of the MBTI® results for each and every administration of the MBTI instrument.

These guidelines are based on a collaborative effort between the Myers and Briggs Foundation, CPP, Inc., the Center for Applications of Psychological Type, CAPT, Inc., and the Association for Psychological Type International, APTi.

PEOPLE TYPES & TIGER STRIPES

The fourth edition of Gordon Lawrence's "gold standard" of books about psychological type.

Offers ideas and insight for improving student achievement by using psychological type in schools.

Includes exercises, charts, tables, and a primer for introducing type effectively into organizations.

PUBLISHED BY THE CENTER FOR APPLICATIONS OF PSYCHOLOGICAL TYPE, INC.
VISIT WWW.CAPT.ORG OR CALL 800-777-2278.

every child appreciated. every child engaged.®

The Murphy-Meisgeier Type indicator for Children® (MMTIC®) assessment was developed specifically to measure psychological type in young people. Used with elementary, middle, and high school students the MMTIC assessment comes with age-specific type reports that address each child's strengths and challenges in school, as well as how they might respond in close relationships.

An easy-to-use online interface facilitates administration for the teacher, educational consultant, or adult who is responsible for the administration of the assessment. Comprehensive support materials are available for all levels, including a career report for middle and high school students. The MMTIC interface is available through www.capt.org.

MURPHY-MEISGEIER **type indicator for children**®

Published by the Center for Applications of Psychological Type, Inc. | www.capt.org | 800-777-2278

discovering type with teens!

Energize and excite teens to learn about themselves
and others with a creative approach to psychological type.
This complete program helps you introduce type
with fun skits, unique exercises, and a step-by-step leader's
guide for presenting workshops.

Includes a Resource CD-ROM with presentations, visuals
and graphics, and reproducible masters.

C A P T

PUBLISHED BY THE CENTER FOR APPLICATIONS OF PSYCHOLOGICAL TYPE, INC.
VISIT WWW.CAPT.ORG OR CALL 800-777-2278.